W. E. B. DU BOIS'S "TALENTED TENTH"

ID Card Exposition Universelle 1900
Department of Special Collections and University Archives,
W. E. B. Du Bois Library, University of Massachusetts Amherst.

A Pioneering Conception of Transformational Leadership | i

> All men cannot go to college but some men must; every isolated group or nation must have its yeast, must have for the talented few centers of training where men are not so mystified and befuddled by the hard and necessary toil of earning a living, as to have no aims higher than their bellies, and no God greater than Gold.
>
> ~ W. E. B. Du Bois

W. E. B. DU BOIS'S "TALENTED TENTH"
A Pioneering Conception of Transformational Leadership

ELLA F. SLOAN, Ed.D.

NIGHT STAR PUBLISHER
San Diego, California

> *A classic is a book that doesn't have to be written again.*
>
> ~ W. E. B. Du Bois

NIGHT STAR PUBLISHER
San Diego, California

Copyright © 2003 by Ella F. Sloan, Ed.D.
All rights reserved

Original manuscript:
Library of Congress Cataloging-in-Publication Data
Registration Number TX 5-699-965
Sloan, Ella F., 1947–
W. E. B. Du Bois's "Talented Tenth": A Pioneering Conception of Transformational Leadership / Ella F. Sloan, Ed.D.

ISBN 978-1-929909-07-0

Cover Photographs
Du Bois as a child and Du Bois as an elderly man:
Department of Special Collections and University Archives, W. E. B. Du Bois Library, University of Massachusetts Amherst.
Du Bois as a young man:
Library of Congress, Prints & Photographs Division, [reproduction number, LC-USZ62-16767] (obtained through wikimedia commons)

Book and Cover Design
Jan Carpenter Tucker, www.nightstarpublisher.com

Dedication

*The force behind my drive,
and empowerment to reach my goals,
has been instilled in me by
the spirit of God,
my mother, Ella M. Hale
and grandmother, Lee Ella Robinson.
I dedicate this book to them, and to
my husband, Winston Sloan,
my daughter, Rhonda Sloan,
my son, Rodney Sloan and
my grandchildren,
Kania, Kaelin, and Kiara.*

❋ *It is the trained, living human soul, cultivated and strengthened by long study and thought, that breathes the real breath of life into boys and girls and makes them human whether they be black or white, Greek, Russian or American.*

~ W. E. B. Du Bois

Contents

Preface   xi

Acknowledgements   xiii

Chapter 1

W. E. B. Du Bois's Challenge to America

Introduction	1
Significance of the Study	3
Statement of the Issue	7
W. E. B. Du Bois Emerges as a Leader	10
Methods	13
Primary Sources	14
Secondary Sources	15
Theoretical Framework	15

Chapter 2

The Historical Development of the "Talented Tenth"

Introduction	23
Alexander Crummell	28

A Pioneering Conception of Transformational Leadership

Philosophical Debate with Booker T. Washington	34
The Negro Academy	54
Prelude to the Niagara Movement	61
The Niagara Movement	64
The National Association for the Advancement of Colored People (NAACP)	71
Summary	88

Chapter 3

The Leadership of W. E. B. Du Bois

Introduction	95
Questions	98
What historical factors led to and influenced Du Bois's development of the Talented Tenth strategy, and what ethical and moral values are implicit within?	98
What light does the Talented Tenth shed on the issue of how transformational leaders are created?	103
How valid are Du Bois's ideas for solving current problems facing the African American community, and how valid is the claim that the Talented Tenth is an integrationist theory?	109
What is the significance of Du Bois's proposal of the Talented Tenth for reconceptualizing the idea of Transformational Leadership, and what can we learn from this theory?	121

Chapter 4
Conclusion 125
    Recommendations 134

References 139

Appendix A
    A Chronology and Life of
    W. E. B. Du Bois 153
    Timeline 155

Appendix B
    The Policy and By-laws of the
    Negro Academy 163

Index 169

About the Author 183

Production Notes 185

Quotations (by first line) 186

> *There is in this world no such force of a person determined to rise. The human soul cannot be permanently chained.*
>
> ~ W. E. B. Du Bois

Preface

In 1903, W. E. B. Du Bois presented a radical leadership proposal for the transformation of African American life in the United States. His theoretical concept of the "Talented Tenth" emphasized the education and training in leadership of ten percent of the African American population. This selective group would transform the larger, uneducated segment of the population and lead them to higher levels of social acceptance and independence.

This study is a historical investigation into the educational ideas of W. E. B. Du Bois's "Talented Tenth." It describes the historical factors that led to and influenced Du Bois's development of the "Talented Tenth" strategy, especially his reaction to and criticism of Booker T. Washington's proposals to accommodate the white power structure through diminished educational and social expectations for African Americans. In contrast to Washington, Du Bois argued that justice and necessity required that blacks receive educational opportunities qualitatively equal to those of whites.

This study finds that many ideas associated with James Burns's notion of "transformational leadership" were anticipated by Du Bois's earlier work, and that scholarship within the field of leadership would benefit from a more inclusive orientation toward the work of minority scholars such as Du Bois.

Du Bois's ideas are analyzed for addressing contemporary problems facing the African American community, and it is concluded that his prescient analyses are still worth reading today. Evidence presented here substantiates not only Du Bois's powerful legacy to African American and general American history, but also shows that the leadership ideas of the "Talented Tenth" were indeed a pioneering conception of Transformational Leadership.

Acknowledgements

In my intellectual journey at the University of San Diego, I have received guidance, support, patience, knowledge, and empathy from my professors: Drs. Steve Gelb, Mary Scherr, and Ronn Johnson. Because of them, I have grown significantly in my academic life. I found the strength to endure and persevere through personal and family illnesses, death, and traumatic life situations and experiences. These challenges have made me a more determined and stronger person. May my professors find here an expression of my sincere gratitude.

Let me express special recognition of Professor Steve Gelb, my dissertation chair, and Mary Scherr, my Academic Advisor. In them, I found teachers of immense dedication and availability. I greatly appreciate their readiness to advise and willingness to assist. Dr. Gelb especially encouraged my work, giving me the time and space to heal without pressure. I learned a great deal from him. I deeply value the professor-student relationship I have had with both my dissertation chair and my academic advisor.

I am indebted to many people in terms of friendship, family, and colleagues. I want to thank all of them. It will not be possible to mention all their names, but let me simply acknowledge my debt of gratitude to my husband, Winston Sloan, who supported me, traveled in and out of the country with me, and assisted me spiritually and financially in my research.

I was generously assisted by certain people in my search for various sources and information on Du Bois. I want to express my appreciation to Linda Seidman and her colleagues of the Department of Special Collections at the University of Massachusetts, Amherst. I also want to thank Dr. Charles Blockson, curator of a special collection of rare and first edition books, manuscripts, and unpublished papers at Temple University in Philadelphia, Pennsylvania. Dr. Blockson graciously opened his private office for several days and allowed me to peruse his collection. I received much encouragement, advice, and insight from Du Bois scholar, Dr. John H. Bracey, Jr., Professor in the W. E. B. Du Bois Department of Afro-American Studies at the University of Massachusetts Amherst and co-director of the documentary on Du Bois. I am equally grateful to Dr. Cornel West, whose lecture I attended at Mesa College. May they find here my deep gratitude.

The following institutions were extremely valuable and helpful in my research: the Schomburg Center for Research in Black Culture in Harlem, New York; the Social Sciences Department of the Library of Congress in Washington D.C.; the Interlibrary Loan

Department of the Copley Library at the University of San Diego; the San Diego State University Special Collections & University Archives, and the W. E. B. Du Bois Memorial Centre for Pan-African Culture in Accra, Ghana.

Finally, I received much clerical, technical, and editorial support from Ellinor Taylor, Jessica Gonzales, Reginald Balintec, and Carol Lemei and Mary Wickline (my editors). This helped to ease my work. May they be assured of my gratitude and friendship.

With the encouragement of numerous colleagues, family members and friends, I have finally realized my dream of developing this dissertation into a book. It is my hope that this form of publication provides a more accessible way to disseminate these important lessons provided by W. E. B. Du Bois's work, life and leadership. May we launch forward yet another generation of leaders.

Dr. Ella F. Sloan

> *Believe in life! Always human beings will live and progress to greater, broader and fuller life.*
> ~ W. E. B. Du Bois

Chapter 1
W. E. B. Du Bois's Challenge to America

✽ Introduction

The "Talented Tenth" was theorized by W. E. B. Du Bois as a strategy to use the best and brightest ten percent of the Negro race. This strategy was presented to college educated Negroes through Du Bois's speeches delivered nationwide at colleges, churches, and community events as a leadership proposal to uplift the race (Green, 1977).

This study explores the historical development of W. E. B. Du Bois's "Talented Tenth" as a foundation of what is now known as Transformational Leadership, which occurs when both leaders and those whom they are guiding are inspired by their relationship to perform at higher levels to effect social change or social benefit. This study also examines the relevance of W. E. B. Du Bois's theories, of training and educating leaders, to college and university Leadership Studies today.

Historical research in education differs from other types of educational research in that the researcher uses data from historical sources such as diaries, published and unpublished documents, and other archival material (Best, 1983; Best & Kahn, 1993). This study reviews and indexes literature, artifacts, photographs, archival documents, personal papers, published and unpublished manuscripts, and rare exhibits that pertain to the life and works of Du Bois. All of these serve as a database for research and as a reference guide for presenting new perspectives and information in the field of Leadership Studies. Writers on transformational leadership incorporate principles similar to those Du Bois followed in the recruiting and training of well-educated Negroes for the "Talented Tenth." This historical review is intended as a blueprint for a change in Leadership Studies that may impact leadership programs significantly in the future. Scholars involved in Leadership Studies and doctoral programs have much to learn from the mainstream of African American leadership.

This historical research focuses upon the following questions:

1. What historical factors led to and influenced Du Bois's development of the "Talented Tenth" strategy, and what ethical and moral values are implicit within it?
2. What light does the "Talented Tenth" shed on the issue of how transformational leaders are created?
3. How valid are Du Bois's ideas for solving current problems facing the African American community, and how valid is the claim that

the "Talented Tenth" is an "integrationist" theory?
4. What is the significance of Du Bois's proposal of the "Talented Tenth" for reconceptualizing the idea of Transformational Leadership, and what can we learn from this theory?

Du Bois's scholarly groundwork began very early. After he received his Ph.D. from Harvard, he taught at Atlanta University from 1897 to 1910. In 1903, Du Bois published his classic book, *The Souls of Black Folk*, in which he criticized African American leader Booker T. Washington (founder of the Tuskegee Institute) for undermining the educational advancement of Negroes by encouraging industrial education rather than academic education. Accepting the call for strong African American leadership, W. E. B. Du Bois confronted the racism of the American social, political, economic, and educational landscape. To accomplish the task of uplifting the American Negro from the very lowest social, political, and economic level, Du Bois strongly believed that a new leadership class was needed, one that required a higher level of academic training and commitment.

❋ Significance of the Study

The concept of the "Talented Tenth" has been widely discussed by contemporary scholars, Lewis (1993, 2000), and Gates and West (1996), who in their discussion gave a great deal of consideration to how Du Bois's ideas had impacted their lives and compelled them to continue to explore his legacy. By taking a closer look at Du Bois's concept of the Talented Tenth, Gates and West conceived of it as both a parable and a leadership paradigm. They also considered themselves to be heirs to the Talented Tenth legacy.

The Talented Tenth (1903b) was Du Bois's major statement on Black leadership. In it, he projected a notion of leadership and leadership development that is frequently used to characterize the whole of his life and work as elitist. The critique focuses on the naming of his system, but the fact of leadership implies an elite—everyone is not a leader.

Unlike *Careers Open to College-Bred Negroes* (Du Bois, 1898/1986), in which he discussed the importance of work, sacrifice, love, and service as the ideals of leadership, Du Bois, in *The Talented Tenth*, focused primarily on demonstrating the correctness of his leadership idea and making clear the relationship between leadership and higher education. In this essay, Du Bois surveyed the great historical figures, both men and women, among American Negroes. He discussed the imperative of increasing the numbers of these men and women as well as methods for doing so. He demonstrated, through the citation of statistics, the lack of educational opportunity that plagued African Americans at that time. Finally, he made an impassioned statement to the American people, urging higher education for talented Negro youths so that they might become inspirational leaders for the remainder of their people. In conclusion, he said:

> Men of America, the problem is plain before you. Here is a race transplanted through the criminal foolishness of your fathers. Whether you like it or not the millions are here, and here they will remain. If you do not lift them up, they will pull you down. Education and work are the levers to uplift a people. Work alone will not do it unless inspired by the right ideals and guided by intelligence. Education must not simply teach work—it must teach Life. The Talented Tenth of the Negro race must be made leaders of thought and missionaries of culture among their people. (Du Bois, 1903b, p. 861)

My study assesses the value of Du Bois's leadership strategies as a vehicle through which African Americans could be led to a level of racial, economic, and social independence. If valid, it will dispel the criticism (Bond, 1925; Davis, 1983; Henderson, 1970) of the "Talented Tenth" as an elitist theory by which only the best and brightest ten percent of African Americans succeed, therefore undermining the remaining ninety percent.

In 1905, Du Bois wrote a historical leadership proposal advocating college training for Negroes, encouraging service and a leadership commitment from the ten percent of blacks who achieved the highest levels of education. He called this new leadership the "Talented Tenth." Du Bois assumed that the ten percent of college-trained and educated individuals like himself would lead the remaining ninety percent of African Americans to liberation and racial uplift—stressing that service was the ideal of leadership.

During the final stage of his life, Du Bois established a close relationship with Ghana's president, Kwame Nkrumah. In 1961, Nkrumah invited Du Bois to relocate to Ghana, where he could live in peace during his final days and use his scholarly skills to help develop an encyclopedia of Africa. While living there in self-imposed exile, Du Bois continued to write scholarly articles and books. He was also very disciplined in writing daily in his diary. He recorded his personal reflections and assessed what he believed to be the most significant leadership accomplishments of his intellectual life. Du Bois became frustrated with the realization that even the leaders of the race, the Talented Tenth, needed more than education to be accepted as equals.

Du Bois lived in Accra, Ghana, from October 1961 until his death on August 27, 1963. Ironically, he died on the eve of the historic March on Washington. Dr. Martin Luther King, Jr. eulogized him at this historical event following the public announcement of his death. Du Bois was buried in Ghana. The Du Bois Memorial Centre for Pan-African Culture is now being used as a shrine for his entombment and as a center for the study of his life and works in Ghana, as well as an educational clearinghouse for studies in education and history.

While living in Africa, Du Bois actively attempted to coordinate a resource network for Africa with France, Germany, Russia, and England, which caused many in the United States government to accuse him of being a communist. However, evidence suggests that Du Bois instead became a Pan-Africanist (advocating African nationalism). In 1968, Du Bois wrote:

> I am not fighting to settle the question of racial equality in America by the process of getting rid of the Negro race. No, what I am fighting for and am still fighting for, is the possibility of black folk and black cultural patterns existing in America without discrimination and on terms of equality. If we take this attitude, we have got to do so consciously and deliberately. (1968b, p. 63)

✻ Statement of the Issue

The field of Leadership Studies in higher education faces many new challenges as learning institutions embark upon the twenty-first century. Leadership training calls for an inclusive and diverse curriculum that is lacking in many educational institutions (Du Bois, 1968a). This study was precipitated by an interest in Leadership Studies in general and, in particular, by curiosity about the reason for the exclusion of African Americans from the leadership curriculum at the college and university level. Du Bois's scholarly works from the late nineteenth century to the early twentieth century present evidence of strong similarities between W. E. B. Du Bois (1903), and James McGregor Burns (1978). This discovery inspired the current exploration of the parallels between the work of these two men in educational leadership. The work of Burns, an Anglo-American scholar, has been incorporated into the curriculum of many institutions, while the work of Du Bois, an African American leader/scholar, is not included in mainstream Leadership Studies.

Du Bois (1903b) proposed the theory of the "Talented Tenth," appealing to exceptional, college-educated black men and women to uplift the black race by making a commitment to work toward educational, economic, and political justice for their fellow black Americans. Interestingly, in 1978, James McGregor Burns criticized the "Great Man Theory" of leadership. It was his view that through relationships with leaders, others could be elevated. Similarly, Du Bois stressed that service was the ideal of leadership (Broderick, 1959; Du Bois, 1903b, 1905, 1911; Moon,

1972). He also viewed higher education as the most efficient and effective pathway toward leadership roles.

Both Burns (1978) and Du Bois (Du Bois, 1903b, 1905a; Lewis, 1995) extensively discussed intellectual and moral leadership. Additionally, Du Bois's scholarly pursuits focused on resolving the Negro problem, which he perceived as resulting from a lack of training and education. In Du Bois's quest to train and develop leaders to solve "The Negro Problem," he challenged his people to put forth their best effort to help themselves. The best way, he believed, was to select and train young Negroes with academic talent to assume the role of the educated Negro leader, who must take responsibility for working to resolve social, racial, political, and economic injustices of the times. Du Bois's notion also led him to believe that integration of the races was the key element to resolving the problem of racial inequality.

Many leadership programs in higher education, unfamiliar with diverse perspectives on leadership, currently rely on Eurocentric perspectives of leadership and base their curriculum on scholars whose perspectives are limited and narrow. For example, my experience with Leadership Studies mostly referenced and used Burns (1978), and Rost (1991), as dominant perspectives of leadership. Little mention is made of African American leaders, past or present, in scholarly writings on leadership.

W. E. B. Du Bois was one of the most prolific of American scholars and historians, and his ideas had a major impact on African American leaders of the late nineteenth and early twentieth century. His pioneering educational and leadership efforts laid the groundwork for the inception of "Transformational Leadership" within the African American community.

✣ W. E. B. Du Bois Emerges as a Leader

W. E. B. Du Bois was gifted intellectually and took pleasure in surpassing his fellow students in academic pursuits. After graduating from high school at the age of 15, he became the local correspondent for the *New York Globe*. He desired to attend Harvard, but could not afford it. Instead, he attended Fisk University in Nashville, Tennessee, where he spent two summers teaching at a country school in order to learn more about the South and his people. There he learned first-hand of poverty, poor soil, ignorance, and prejudice. But, more importantly, he learned that his people had a deep desire for knowledge. Du Bois was eventually able to commence his graduate studies at Harvard, where, in 1896, he was the first African American to receive a doctoral degree. Afterwards, he studied abroad at the University of Berlin in Germany for two years. While in Berlin, he began to see more clearly the race problems that existed in Africa and

America. His doctoral thesis, *The Suppression of the African Slave Trade to the United States of America: 1638-1870*, (Du Bois, 1896) remains one of the most authoritative works on that subject and is the first volume in Harvard's Historical Series. With his schooling behind him at the age of 26, he began his life's work. He accepted a teaching job at Wilberforce University in Ohio, turning down offers from the Lincoln Institute in Missouri and Tuskegee Institute in Alabama (Du Bois, 1968b).

In 1896, after graduating from Harvard, Du Bois plunged eagerly into his research. He was certain that the underachievement of black people was not due to lack of ability, but to deep-seated racial prejudice. This helped fuel his determination to unearth as much knowledge as he could in order to find a "cure" for color prejudice. In 1899, he published *The Philadelphia Negro*, a sociological study, which demonstrated that the inequality of the Negro in America was a symptom of deep social and economic problems. He presented African Americans as a striving, energetic group, not an inert body of criminals as he had once suspected (Du Bois, 1899).

During this period, an ideological controversy between Du Bois and Booker T. Washington began, which later grew into a bitter personal debate. Washington argued that black people should temporarily forgo political power, insistence on civil rights, and higher education for Negro youths.

Instead, he believed they should concentrate on learning industrial and vocational skills. In a 1903 speech he said, "Cast down your bucket wherever you are," a statement encouraging blacks to build on skills they had so they could get jobs, rather than acquiring higher education. This approach angered W. E. B. Du Bois and he labeled Washington an accommodationist and an "Uncle Tom" (Du Bois, 1903a). Du Bois was not opposed to Washington's power—grants, job placement, proposals, and many endeavors concerning blacks were sent to Washington for endorsement or rejection; making the "Tuskegee Machine" the focal point for black political power—but he disagreed with Washington's ideology, principles, and methodology. Du Bois believed in his concept of the "Talented Tenth," who, through their knowledge and expertise in their various fields, could lead the American Negro into a higher level of acceptance in America, to political and economic rights, and thus, liberation.

In discussing the heart and soul of W. E. B. Du Bois's educational thought, Wilentz (1994) described him as an integrationist with a double consciousness, who straddled the fence between integration into American society and Pan-Africanism (the movement promoting all black people in the African diaspora). Du Bois was a man with stark polarities and huge contradictions, and a humanitarian who worked actively for the cause of equality between the sexes as well as racial equality.

Numerous biographies have been written on W. E. B. Du Bois (Aptheker 1968, 1993; Broderick, 1959; Du Bois 1952, 1968; Woodard, 1976). Some portray him as a trail-blazing scholar who recognized his own brilliance. Some present him as deserving the credit for developing mainstream Leadership Studies (Byerman 1994; Gates & West, 1996; Lewis, 1996)

❋ Methods

The basic research method used in this book was historical inquiry, which involved the investigation of primary and secondary sources. The goal of historical research is to treat evidence fairly by searching for the overall pattern in historical events and by producing compelling analytical conclusions. My research accessed published and unpublished documents, oral communication, preserved artifacts, historical events, and biographies of W. E. B. Du Bois. I also catalogued the work of scholars who have referenced the works of Du Bois in order to analyze his influence upon current Leadership Studies. I examined prior and current assumptions that pertained to Du Bois's leadership strategies for social change and racial equality through education, in addition to his ideas for attempting to implement such concepts in meeting the needs of the black community (Du Bois, 1903b, 1905, 1968a, 1968b).

The purpose of this study is to produce new information relevant to the field of educational leadership. The historical research method enabled me to develop a conceptual framework for Du Bois's idea of the "Talented Tenth" and show how the strategies utilized by Du Bois to enlist and train his "Talented Tenth" were actually an early version of Transformational Leadership (Du Bois, 1903b, 1968a; West, 1982).

❋ Primary Sources

Du Bois wrote more than twenty books, hundreds of articles, many editorials, and even poems that set forth his political, economic, social, and educational beliefs. His published and unpublished papers provide a wealth of information about him, his family, his education, his views on the problems of African Americans, and his outlook on human problems at the national and global level. The University of Massachusetts's Special Collection at Amherst, the Charles L. Blockson Afro-American Collection at Temple University Library in Philadelphia, Pennsylvania, the Library of Congress in Washington, D.C., the Schomburg Center for Research in Black Culture in Harlem, and local libraries in San Diego, along with my travels to Ghana, West Africa, provided valuable research findings. Other valuable data was gained through video documentaries, exhibits, and personal conversations with Du Bois scholars: University of Massachusetts Amherst's Professor John Bracey and Temple University's Charles Blockson.

⁂ Secondary Sources

I explored related literature and compared the analyses of present scholars of Du Bois's work to that of earlier scholars. Particular attention was given to implications for Leadership Studies for the twenty-first century. I reviewed the work of contemporary scholars such as David Levering Lewis, Henry Louis Gates, Jr., Cornel West, Andrew Paschal, and S. P. Fallinwider, with an eye toward understanding Du Bois's ideas in the context of current studies on how leaders can be educated.

⁂ Theoretical Framework

"The Talented Tenth" is a theoretical concept emphasizing education and leadership training of a selected ten percent of the African American population, who could then uplift the race as a whole. Du Bois (1905, 1911) referred to the "Talented Tenth" as a means to an end. Fundamental to his concept was his formula using selective criteria to enlist his cadre of leaders (Broderick, 1959; Logan, 1971).

Although the notion of Transformational Leadership is associated with James McGregor Burns's

1978 work, *Leadership*, W. E. B. Du Bois articulated a similar vision near the turn of the century. In writing of the need for social regeneration in the American black community, he argued that:

> The responsibility for their own social regeneration ought to be placed largely upon the shoulders of the Negro people. But such responsibility must carry with it a grant of power; responsibility without power is a mockery and farce. If, therefore, the American people are sincerely anxious that the Negro shall put forth his best efforts to help himself, they must see to it that he is not deprived of the freedom and power to strive. (Du Bois, 1903, p. 21)

This quote parallels Burns's (1978) theory, because it emphasizes the empowerment of followers through transformational processes.

Burns (1978) discussed leadership as transforming, and on occasion, as transformational. By definition, Burns described transforming leadership as morally uplifting. Du Bois (1903, 1905) suggested leaders are transforming when they uplift their race. In order for this to occur, he stated that the college educated ten percent have both a moral and social responsibility to train the other 90 percent. Doing what is right, good, and important would help foster a higher level of achievement. The truly transformational leader, according to Du Bois (1903, 1905), is a leader who is seeking the greatest good for the greatest number and is concerned about doing what is right and honest, thus setting an example for the followers.

Du Bois (1903b) and Burns (1978) are more different than they are alike. The differences are rooted in their theories, for example, Du Bois's theory of the Talented Tenth is race based, and his appeal for leadership was directed to African American college graduates. Whereas, Burns's theory of transformational leadership is grounded in the process of a mutual relationship, and primarily appeals to mainstream leaders.

Both Du Bois (1903b, 1905) and Burns (1978) are scholars with similar philosophical views and both view leadership and power as a source of relationship, central to achieving the goal and necessary in meeting the fundamental needs of the followers. However, Burns (1978, p. 12) suggested that power must be analyzed in the context of motives and resources; and that the nature of leadership requires the understanding of power and the intention for mutuality. Du Bois (1903b) suggested that power and leadership need to be trusted to the best and the brightest of the race for the good of uplifting the masses, which required education for understanding. Du Bois's (1905) criteria for leadership required college education and training. Burns and Du Bois wear different masks for different occasions or reasons, both believing themselves to be authorities on leadership. What is to be noted here is that Burns's view presents power as a mutually beneficial and dynamic interaction between both parties (leader and follower) as opposed to the more traditional view of power as being a one-sided, dominating, and hierarchical relationship. In contrast, Du Bois's view was both traditional and broad in his approach to leadership, he viewed power through education, training and an inclusive democracy. Although enriching and meaningful, it was designed to create a structure of economic independence and freedom for both the followers and leaders.

Burns (1978) indicated that intellectual leaders of the 18th and 19th centuries seem to have been driven by internal conflict that expressed itself in emotional breakdowns, withdrawals, or alienations. The life of an intellectual leader is inherently conflict ridden and is magnified by the social and political environment.

Burns (1978) noted that an intellectual leader is a moralist. He stated that intellectual leaders deal with both analytical and normative ideas, and that they bring both to bear on their environment. Intellectual leaders are not detached from their social milieu. Intellectual leadership is transforming leadership (Burns, 1978, p. 142). Burns defined the intellectual ideologist as a person in a particular cultural milieu or a social class. An intellectual is, in the first sense, described by Burns as a devotee to ideas, values, and knowledge and is creative with a contemplative state of mind. An intellectual is a person concerned critically with values and purposes that transcend immediate practical needs.

Black intellectuals have always operated in a shifting environment of crisis regarding the need to fight the influence of Social Darwinism, uplift the masses through accommodation or assimilation strategies, fight for the acknowledgement of their voices, and break through institutional barriers that force them to define their right to study issues that go beyond race. Du Bois (1903, 1908, 1920) suggested that if leaders are to lead, they must be politically and morally committed to changing the social and racial order (Black Scholars, 2001, p. 3). According to Burns's (1978) definition of intellectual leader/leadership within a political context, Du Bois will qualify on the basis of being a social reformer, with a desire to elevate his race and mankind, endeavoring to improve the condition of mankind and to impact change. In other words, by comparison, Du Bois's notion of intellectual leadership responsibility went beyond Burns's idea.

Du Bois's leadership proposal and his controversial ideas have challenged both scholars and leaders throughout the twentieth century. Past scholars and researchers spoke with passion of the mission of the great orator of the twentieth century. Bond (1925), Clifford (1903), Hastie (1934), and Scarborough (1903) describe Du Bois as a great philosopher, writer, and visionary, one who accurately predicted that the problem of the twentieth century would be the color line and dubbed Du Bois as an intellectual giant who used his skills to agitate the correction of injustice against his people. West (1993) stated that his lectures on Du Bois in his cultural studies left him "exhausted and exhilarated," primarily because Du Bois's twentieth century articulation of the problem of the color line haunted him in such a way that it became a fundamental challenge to his aim in life.

Art is not simply works of art; it is the spirit that knows Beauty, that has music in its soul and the color of sunsets in its handkerchief, that can dance on a flaming world and make the world dance too.

~ W. E. B. Du Bois

❋ *The cost of liberty is less than the price of repression.*

~ W. E. B. Du Bois

Chapter 2
The Historical Development of the "Talented Tenth"

❈ Introduction

An author, journalist, social reformer, poet, philosopher and educator, W. E. B. Du Bois wielded one of the most influential pens in African American history. For sixty-six years he functioned not only as a mentor, model, and spokesman for generations of black Americans who yearned for racial equality, but also as the conscience of white Americans (V. P. Franklin, 1995). In his 1903 address, "The Talented Tenth," Du Bois challenged the Negro race. He urged Negroes to accept the responsibility of prioritizing their lives. More importantly, he urged Negroes to join the movement to fight for three issues: first, for political power for Negro citizens; second, for insistence on civil rights for Negroes; and third, for higher education for Negro youths. "Education and work are the levers to uplift a people. Work alone will not do it unless inspired by the right ideals and guided by intelligence. Education must not simply teach work—it must teach Life" (Du Bois, 1903b, p. 861).

According to Moon (1968, 1972), Mandela (1994), and Lester (1971), W. E. B. Du Bois was one of the most brilliant and prolific black authors of the 20th century. More than any other individual, Du Bois developed a philosophy that set the goals for freedom and intellectualism in the black world. A scholar of vast erudition and eclectic interests, Du Bois's writings touched every aspect of African American culture, ranging from education to Pan-Africanism and from art to religion. The education of Negro youths at home and abroad was a topic of never-ending concern to him. In his long career he was cast into many roles, including leader, philosopher, and editor. But always and essentially, he was a teacher. He considered education a key to solving the vexatious color problem—more and better education at all levels and for each according to his individual capacity (Moon, 1972).

Du Bois's 1903 memorial speech, addressed to the college graduates at Atlanta University, appealed to college trained Negroes, inviting them to join his leadership task force, the Talented Tenth. (Du Bois, 1903b). It was a lifetime theme, which he believed was the most appropriate path toward the advancement of black people. He believed the best way to develop black leadership was to select and educate the most talented and capable of black youths so that they could mentor others and break the cycle of poverty and lack of education, which defined the lives of most African

Americans. His thinking along these lines stands out as one of his most significant theoretical contributions. It is perhaps his most elaborately developed and one that remained remarkably consistent throughout his career. This leadership theory has been traced back to as early as 1891 when Du Bois, a student at Harvard, deplored the South's effort to make common and industrial schools, rather than colleges, the basis of its educational system for black youths.

Du Bois (1903b) argued that progress for black people had been hindered at times by two *mistaken* notions. "First that no more could ever rise save the few already risen; second, that it would be better the unrisen to pull the risen down" (Du Bois, 1903b, p. 847). Du Bois (1903b, 1924) maintained that the process of uplifting black Americans must be accomplished primarily by means of providing them with education and employment. Training of the Talented Tenth would be the means to ensure political and civil rights for black Americans equal to those enjoyed by white Americans. In Dr. Joy James's (1997) opinion, Du Bois's speech, "The Talented Tenth," is a classic leadership proposal with twenty-first century implications. It articulated a model of leadership for the black community. James also noted that Du Bois's proposal in "The Talented Tenth" has historical seeds in one century and consequences in another, and she pointed out that Du Bois was not the only leader with an idea to select the best and brightest. Other voices existed: Ella Baker, Frantz Fanon, Ida B. Wells (and many others) are some who played a substantial role in uplifting the race. James's concern was the behavior of the black intelligentsia: Were those educated as part of the Talented Tenth uplifting others as Du Bois intended, or were they climbing only for themselves, as others believed?

Past and contemporary scholars have indicated that Du Bois's leadership notion of "The Talented Tenth" was influenced by the American Negro Academy and by his mentor Alexander Crummell, who himself was an accomplished scholar and Episcopalian minister. Du Bois's speech "The Talented Tenth" was also developed as a rebuttal to Booker T. Washington's Tuskegee Machine, which Du Bois viewed as accommodationist. Du Bois disagreed with Washington's call for Negroes to apply themselves to hard work at whatever manual jobs were available to them and to forego aspirations for civil rights and higher education for Negro youths. Du Bois's speech proposed a very different approach to the Negro problem. He believed that social development and respect for American Negroes could only be achieved through better education (Brody, 1972; Childs, 1989; Davis, 1983). As an educator, Du Bois devised the concept of the "Talented Tenth" as a way of raising the social and economic status of black people. It was during his teaching career at Wilberforce, Atlanta, and Pennsylvania Universities that Du Bois began to

inspire many young men and women of the Negro race to enlist in his Talented Tenth force. Du Bois (1903) maintained that, in time of crisis such as African Americans were facing:
> the most capable and cultural men of all races must join hands for the sake of human history and provide leadership, in thought and action, and to make a difference in uplifting the masses and lead them to a place of respectability. On this foundation, we shall build bread winning, skill of hand and quickness of brain, which have the ability to make the difference between catastrophe and salvation. (p. 38)

This chapter will discuss the historical development of the "Talented Tenth" as Du Bois's attempt to solve the Negro problem. It will demonstrate the influence of Du Bois's mentor, Alexander Crummell, and his Negro Academy, upon Du Bois in his search of men with potential for higher education, and in his struggle to establish a creed and criteria for selecting leadership. It will highlight the historical events which shaped the evolving leadership of the men and women who comprised the Talented Tenth, including the philosophical debate between Du Bois and Booker T. Washington, and the significance of The Niagara Movement as the early incarnation of the National Association for the Advancement of Colored People (NAACP).

✳ Alexander Crummell

Gates and West (1996) noted that Alexander Crummell, a noted black intellectual, influenced Du Bois's Talented Tenth idea. Alexander Crummell is still unknown to most Americans, although he has begun as of late to reappear in scholarly examinations of African American history. In Du Bois's 1903 classic, *The Souls of Black Folk,* Du Bois wrote of Alexander Crummell: "His name to-day, in this broad land, means little, and comes to fifty million ears laden with no incense of memory or emulation. And herein lies the tragedy of the age ... " (Du Bois, 1903a, p. 178). Du Bois's lament is just as appropriate today as it was eighty years ago. Crummell, despite his powerful will and his undaunted love for his people, failed to impress his name on their consciousness.

Rigsby (1987) tells a great deal about the life of this remarkable man. He describes the depth of historical, educational, religious, and racial forces that helped to shape Crummell and which in turn were influenced by him. Rigsby asserts that, though not completely forgotten, Crummell has no major place in black history texts or literary anthologies. There is a need for reappraisal of this great scholar-leader who should be better known and whose name should have its place in history. Dr. Rigsby has returned to history a great intellectual leader. His research has rescued Crummell from semi-oblivion and has placed him among the black pioneer intellectuals who influenced the course of black life in America.

Crummell's life falls into four distinct periods: (1) 1819-1847: his training in America; (2) 1847-1853: his education in England; (3) 1853-1873: his missionary work for black people in Africa; and (4) 1873-1898: his final years of influence in America (Meier, 1966; Wahle, 1968).

Born free in New York City on March 3,1819, Alexander Crummell was the son of Boston Crummell, a self-emancipated black born in Africa, and Charity Hicks, an African American whose family had lived free in the United States for several generations.

Alexander Crummell completed his early education at New York's African Free School and at Canal Street High School, both operated by African American clergymen. He completed his secondary education at Oneida Institute in Whitesboro, New York, which was run by black and white abolitionists. Oneida combined studies of the classics with manual labor, a simultaneously intellectual and practical approach to life that Crummell would employ the rest of his years. Crummell graduated from Oneida in 1839.

Crummell wished to study for the priesthood, but received many rebuffs because he was black. He was later ordained in the Diocese of Massachusetts, Episcopal Church in 1844. He studied in England where he graduated from Queens College in 1853.

Crummell was the first African American to earn a bachelor's degree from the University of Cambridge. In 1895, Crummell taught theology at Howard University, where he expanded his views on the importance of Liberal Arts and vocational education. As an Episcopalian minister he served twenty years in Liberia, West Africa (V. P. Franklin, 1995).

The *Liberia Records of Letter* (January 31, 1972) asserted that Crummell saw no dichotomy between the practical and the ideal, the pragmatic and the mystical. However, it was the busy world of practical affairs that dominated most of his life in Liberia. For example, soon after his arrival in Liberia, he expressed concerns that a church needed to be built at once in Monrovia. The establishment of a church, which was to serve as a meeting place for black unity, became central to the Christian Pan-African concept.

Crummell's resignation from his foreign mission occurred because events unfolded that were contrary to his Pan-African plans. He had come to Liberia eager to offer, in the ecclesiastical sphere, the black leadership that the nation enjoyed in the political arena. He understood that there could be no effective Christian Pan-African movement unless black people assumed the highest leadership roles in the church and state. However, the loyal Episcopal clergymen were not prepared to establish an independent black church in Liberia. This was inconsistent with Crummell's "principle oneness" (Schomberg collection of John E.

Bruce's papers, letter dated Jan., 1894). He continued his activities after his return to the U. S. in 1872 (V. P. Franklin, 1995). He died peacefully on September 10, 1898, in Point Pleasant, New Jersey.

Crummell was a well-published intellectual. In 1861, he published *The Relations and Duties of Free Colored Men in America to Africa* and in 1862, *The Future of Africa.* In these works, he argued that blacks around the world shared a common experience of racial discrimination. In 1882, he published a collection of sermons called *The Greatness of Christ,* in which he argued that Christians could not find salvation merely by accepting Christ but that they must also work constantly for the good of humanity.

In 1897, he co-founded the Negro Academy in an effort to give shape to black intellectualism and to counter the rising discrimination and segregation of the late nineteenth century. Crummell anticipated the great debate between Booker T. Washington and W. E. B. Du Bois, (Crummell was a role model and mentor for Du Bois).

Crummell's life spanned almost the entire nineteenth century and was distinguished by his intellectual achievements and missionary work, but his was not a blameless life. Moses (1989) noted that in his youth, Crummell was influenced to become morally rigid and isolated in response to racial insults and prejudice. This made him bitter and resentful. He had difficulty making and retaining friendships (whether black or white). There were some who found his lifestyle unbearable, including his wife and children. This led to divorce. Furthermore, his children deserted him in his old age, and his son refused to attend his funeral. According to V. P. Franklin (1995), Crummell often offended others with his domineering, possessive behavior, which most African Americans found difficult to endure. He was considered uncompromising, authoritative and almost autocratic in his racial beliefs (Rigsby, 1987).

Moses (1989) asserted that Alexander Crummell was such a conservative elitist and intellectual leader, that he fit neither the academic nor popular stereotype of black culture. He believed that humanity was caught in a life and death struggle with powerful forces of nature, capable of reducing mankind to savagery unless kept under strictest control.

Crummell was among the most prolific writers and intellectuals who kept alive the tradition of emphasizing moral uprightness as the basis of racial greatness throughout the 19th century, and he passed it along to such literary heirs as W. E. B. Du Bois. Yet, unlike Du Bois, Washington, and other scholars of the past whose texts are widely available, Crummell's speeches and publications remained inaccessible until recently. For the first time, John Oldfield (1995), a lecturer at the University of Southampton, provided a thorough scholarly edition of Crummell's most significant writings on the south, entitled *Civilization and Black Progress: Selected Writings of Alexander Crummell on the South, 1819 - 1898.* Additionally, Oldfield (1995) prefaced each address with a concise statement of Crummell's work as a whole and made clear his voice on race relations and the need for Negro institutions, such as: Negro colleges, Negro businesses, a Negro school of literature and art, and Negro newspapers. He believed these institutions would serve as an intellectual clearinghouse for the nurturing of Negro minds (Du Bois, 1903, 1911, 1925; Scarborough, 1903).

According to Rigsby (1987), Crummell's vision was the precursor of the much later theory of the Talented Tenth. Two facts can be gleaned from this statement. First, and perhaps the most important, is that Crummell believed in a superior class of black men. Second, he believed in the powers of educated black men to uplift the race through the training standards for black youths.

Crummell was an intellectual, a teacher, a scholar, a black Episcopalian minister, a missionary, an abolitionist, and a man of letters knowledgeable in classics at a time when the average black was an illiterate slave (Du Bois, 1903b, 1905). He was an outspoken critic of racial injustice and the exclusion of African American people from the mainstream of American society. There is no question about his brilliance as a writer or his capacity for original thought. His life symbolizes the intricacy of the black

American experience. Crummell represented many intellectuals with their conflicting emotions regarding the Western World, their discontent with "civilization" and their dependency on it as they labored to impose order on their existence both as racial beings and as individuals (Moses, 1989). Crummell encouraged African Americans to recognize their common experience. He played a major role in shaping African American intellectual thought. Crummell's interests and experiences in the West African country of Liberia were widely recognized. An innovative and effective educator, and a Christian mystic, Alexander Crummell was, above all else, a seminal figure who foreshadowed a diverse group of leaders including Booker T. Washington, W. E. B. Du Bois, and Marcus Garvey (Rigsby, 1987).

✸ Philosophical Debate with Booker T. Washington

From the early nineteenth century to the beginning of the new millennium, African Americans argued about how best to survive, confront, and succeed against racism as it existed in America. At the turn of the century, this historical dilemma was known by the African American community as the "Great Debate," a philosophical and political prizefight between two brilliant educators and orators, W. E. B. Du Bois and Booker T. Washington (Frazier, 1928).

These conflicting points of view are today reflected in the divergent beliefs of the new Talented Tenth leaders, including Republican Congressman, J. C. Watts of Oklahoma and Clarence Thomas, Supreme Court Justice, who both were recipients of, but are against, affirmative action and social policy as it relates to the uplifting of the race. Reverend Jesse Jackson of Operation Push in Chicago, and Colin Powell, Secretary of Defense in the Bush administration are advocates of affirmative action and social policy. Both utilize their positions of leadership to uplift the race. These opposing viewpoints have created a controversial issue in the political arena.

Over one hundred years ago, Booker T. Washington was catapulted to national fame as a result of his speech in Atlanta at the Southern Cotton Exposition on September 18, 1895. It was the first time in Southern history that a black man had been invited to speak before an audience of white notables. His speech had great appeal to the white industrialists and politicians sharing the stage with him.

This angered Du Bois (1903a) because Washington was assuring white leaders that blacks could participate in American economic and industrial development without threat to the established social order. Their argument was based on how best to "uplift" the Negro race and how to solve the "Negro problem."

In the "Atlanta Compromise," Washington (1901) lauded the white organizers and proclaimed to speak for black people. He spoke in parables to black people telling them effectively to stay where they were (implying their station in life):

> Mr. President and Gentlemen of the Board of Directors and Citizens:
>
> One-third of the population of the South is of the Negro race. No enterprise seeking the material, civil, or moral welfare of this section can disregard this element of our population and reach the highest success. I but convey to you, Mr. President and Directors, the sentiment of the masses of my race when I say that in no way have the value and manhood of the American Negro been more fittingly and generously recognized than by the managers of this magnificent Exposition at every stage of its progress. It is a recognition that will do more to cement the friendship of the two races than any occurrence since the dawn of our freedom.
>
> Not only this, but the opportunity here afforded will awaken among us a new era of industrial progress. Ignorant and inexperienced, it is not strange that in the first years of our new life we began at the top instead of at the bottom; that a seat in Congress or the state legislature was more sought than real estate or industrial skill; that the political convention or stump speaking

had more attractions than starting a dairy farm or truck garden.

A ship lost at sea for many days suddenly sighted a friendly vessel. From the mast of the unfortunate vessel was seen a signal, "Water, water; we die of thirst!" The answer from the friendly vessel at once came back, "Cast down your bucket where you are." A second time the signal, "Water, water; send us water!" ran up from the distressed vessel, and was answered, "Cast down your bucket where you are." And a third and fourth signal for water was answered, "Cast down your bucket where you are." The captain of the distressed vessel, at last heeding the injunction, cast down his bucket, and it came up full of fresh, sparkling water from the mouth of the Amazon River.

To those of my race who depend on bettering their condition in a foreign land or who underestimate the importance of cultivating friendly relations with the Southern white man, who is their next-door neighbor, I would say: "Cast down your bucket where you are"—cast it down in making friends in every manly way of the people of all races by whom we are surrounded.

Cast it down in agriculture, mechanics, in commerce, in domestic service, and in the professions. And in this connection it is well to bear in mind that whatever other sins the South may be called to bear, when it comes to business, pure and simple, it is in the South that the Negro is given a man's chance in the commercial world, and in nothing is this Exposition more eloquent than in emphasizing this chance. Our greatest danger is that in the great leap from slavery to freedom we may overlook the fact that the masses of us are to live by the productions of our hands, and fail to keep in mind that we shall prosper in proportion as we learn to dignify and glorify common labor, and put brains and skill into the common occupations of life; shall prosper in proportion as we learn to draw the line between the superficial and the substantial, the ornamental gewgaws of life and the useful. No race can prosper till it learns that there is as much dignity in tilling a field as in writing a poem. It is at the bottom of life we must begin, and not at the top. Nor should we permit our grievances to overshadow our opportunities ... "Cast down your bucket where you are!" (Washington, 1901, pp. 218-220)

Out of the despair of the 1890s, Washington emerged as one of the most powerful black men ever to operate on the American scene. Born into slavery about 1858, he was a man of driving ambition and obvious ability. By 1895, when he made his famous Atlanta Exposition address, he had achieved national prominence. Washington decided to concentrate on the traits that "decent whites were prepared to allow black men to develop." He emphasized thrift, hard work, self-help, and industrial education and played down political and social rights. From his base as principal of Tuskegee Normal and Industrial Institute in Alabama, Washington tried to direct the affairs of black men in America (Du Bois, 1903, 1909; Ferris, 1913; Scarborough, 1903).

Frazier (1957) asserted that Booker T. Washington rose to prominence in 1895 as a leader of Negroes through his apparent acceptance of racial segregation as a solution to "the Negro Problem." Under his leadership, financial and political support for "Industrial Education" for Negroes was provided by northern capitalists. This support occurred at a crucial time: when lynchings and mob violence were used to put the Negro in his or her place in the south. During this period, many gave up their hopes for freedom and equality in American life.

Equality and education were the primary topics of controversy in the debate between Du Bois and Washington. In 1903, W. E. B. Du Bois, challenging Washington as spokesman for the black community, published the essay "Of Mr. Booker T. Washington and Others" (Du Bois, 1903a, p. 38-51). It was the first public sign of Du Bois's growing disagreement with Washington, with whom he had worked earlier on various projects (Du Bois, 1904, 1905).

Du Bois wrote in "Of Mr. Booker T. Washington and Others" (1903a), "Washington represents in Negro thought the old attitude of adjustment and submission; but adjustments at such a peculiar time as to make his program unique" (1903a, p. 44). Du Bois and Washington engaged themselves in a fierce battle—a battle based on their different ideological premises. This conflict never resulted in a face to face debate. Rather, it manifested itself as an acerbic exchange of ideas via correspondence, speeches, writings, newspaper articles, and refuting each other's theories through chapters in books.

For example, Du Bois (1903a) began in his essay on Washington in *The Souls of Black Folk*:

> Easily the most striking thing in the history of the American Negro since 1876 is the ascendancy of Mr. Booker T. Washington. It began at the time when war memories and ideals were rapidly passing; a day of astonishing commercial development was dawning; a sense of doubt and hesitation overtook the freedmen's sons,—then it was that his leading began. Mr. Washington came, with a simple definite programme...his program of industrial education. (p. 38)

Booker T. Washington, the founder and President of the Tuskegee Institute (now Tuskegee University) was, indeed, the most powerful and influential black man in America from the mid 1890s to his death in 1915. White businessmen and political leaders readily sought his advice and counsel on virtually every issue impacting black people.

Washington (1895) wanted to educate, but never in a way that would be threatening to white America. By building an economic base first, Washington believed that Negroes would gain acceptance and dignity and should be satisfied with separate but equal concessions. Washington's leadership influence was stronger during his time than was that of Du Bois. Washington had the ear and purse of influential white philanthropists such as the Carnegies and Rockefellers.

In 1903, it was clear, though, that Washington's greatest competition for the leadership of the black community would come from the brilliant and aggressive W. E. B. Du Bois. Du Bois, the first black person to receive a Ph.D. from Harvard, had as his original ambition to make a complete study of the history and present condition of black people in America. Although he had worked with Washington on several projects in the first years of the century, Du Bois found Washington's lack of flexibility and unwillingness to accept criticism a barrier to further cooperation.

Du Bois (1968a) found Washington's positions and unbridled power repugnant and reprehensible.

Du Bois stated that "I was increasingly uncomfortable under the statements of Mr. Washington's position." Du Bois wrote further, in his autobiography, of his discomfort with Washington's "depreciation of the value of the vote; his dislike of Negro colleges; and his general attitude which seemed to place the blame for the status of Negroes upon the Negroes themselves rather than upon the whites" (1968a, p. 240). Du Bois explained his reasoning, "I was greatly disturbed at this time, not because I was in absolute opposition to the things that Mr. Washington was advocating, but because I was strongly in favor of more agitation against wrongs" (p. 242).

Ferris (1913), Field (1909), and Du Bois (1902), later wrote that Du Bois became increasingly suspicious of the power enjoyed by Washington as a result of the financial support that he received from the white community. Du Bois (1903b, 1968a) noted that, though Washington had spoken in 1895 of increased support and cooperation between the races, the end of the century had brought the disenfranchisement of black people and increased color discrimination. Du Bois (1897, 1903, 1905) called for criticism by blacks of Washington's program of accommodation, or adapting to the existing situation. According to Du Bois (1903, 1905), Washington was holding back the development of the "Talented Tenth" of black youths who were capable of competing on equal terms with whites and discouraging black men from insisting on natural and civil rights necessary to their advancement.

Ferris (1913) noted that Du Bois argued that a man is not the slave of circumstances, but transforms his environment after the pattern of his ideals. He recognized that a man by his own attitude may transform the world's estimate of him. Whether Du Bois was right or wrong, he was following in the footsteps of his mentor, Alexander Crummell.

Ferris (1913) stated in his "Gospel of Work," that Washington emphasized a basic law of human progress. Ferris (1913) also noted that Washington's policy was to recognize race prejudice as a fundamental fact, just as one recognizes the law of gravity as a basic law of nature. Washington's advice was to buckle down to hard work, not rock the boat, and everything would come out all right in the long run.

It was a rash man who dared criticize Washington's theories. Washington was entrenched behind the protective gates of Tuskegee, where he was safe against criticism. He and his work were so strongly connected that to criticize his theories seemed an attack on him (Crummell, 1898; Du Bois, 1897; Ferris, 1913).

Du Bois's (1897, 1903) crusading zeal for humanity, justice, and civil rights evolved as one of the most powerful promotions for the black man's social enfranchisement within an atmosphere against racial development. Du Bois was criticized for desiring the social as well as the civil and political recognition of the colored man. Meanwhile, Du Bois was formulating his notion of leadership by a college educated elite, which he regarded as necessary for the advancement of any group (Du Bois 1897, 1901, 1903b). He thought that the educated elite had a greater opportunity to guide the race by reshaping its own ideals in order to provide the masses with appropriate goals and lift them to civilization.

Like Washington (1895, 1901), Du Bois (1897, 1902, 1903b) combined an enthusiasm for racial solidarity with one for economic development and middle class virtues. In 1897, Du Bois's speaking on "The Conservation of Races," was more emphatic about the value of racial integrity, than any other time during this period; and asserted that there existed subtle psychic differences that divided men into races. He regarded the "race spirit" as "the most ingenious invention for human progress" (Du Bois, 1897, p. 817). "The Negroes inspired by one vast ideal can work out in its fullness the great message we have for humanity" (Du Bois, 1897, p. 820).

Washington and Du Bois had come to disagree not only in their educational philosophy, but also on the fundamental question of the immediate importance of the ballot. By 1903, Du Bois was not only pleading for higher education, but had begun to criticize the work of industrial schools. Both men spoke to captains of industry: the Tuskegeean emphasized economic skills, the Atlanta educator stressed a high grade of culture. Miller's essays on "Race Adjustment" (1909) asserted that Du Bois "had never betrayed his race, in public utterances or in written article, in his zeal for equal opportunity and equal rights" (pp. 146, 148-149). Samuel Spencer's (1955) article on "Booker T. Washington and the Negro's Place in American Life" carried a different tone. Washington's influence over the press and his soft pedaling of agitation on segregation and disenfranchisement was viewed as being deplorable.

By 1905, Du Bois had definitely come to a parting of the ways with Washington. In the pages of *The Crisis* (1911, 1914) and *The Horizon* (1907) one can best observe Du Bois as the consistent agitator and the ardent and brilliant fighter for integration and citizenship rights. He insisted, for example, that disenfranchisement inhibited the economic development of the Negro because the inability to vote affected their ability to protect their property rights. Du Bois, scholar and prophet, mystic and materialist, ardent agitator for political rights and propagandist for economic cooperation denounced segregation and called for integration into American society in accordance with the principles of human brotherhood and the ideals of democracy.

Washington, however, appealing to his white audience, reminded them of what he called the familiarity and faithfulness of the southern black man. Rejecting social equality as an immediate goal,

Washington instead spoke of building a new south through agricultural and industrial cooperation between the races (Du Bois, 1897). Newspapers in all parts of the United States had published Washington's "Atlanta Compromise" address in full, and for months afterwards, there were complimentary editorial references to Washington's speech as being the best ever in character and in warmth of its reception. His fame, power, and control of the purse strings grew.

Crummell challenged Du Bois to oppose Washington's ideas of the "Atlanta Compromise" and to organize black intellectuals to become thinkers and leaders for the Negro race. Crummell (1898) excluded Booker T. Washington from the American Negro Academy and disregarded Washington himself as a leader of the race. Crummell mentored Du Bois and labeled Washington an accommodationist. Du Bois was embraced as visionary.

Classic scholars like Crummell, Du Bois, and Trotter (a journalist) set the stage for contemporary black intellectuals and scholars. Gates and West (1996) are constructing a new platform for black America through which Du Bois and Washington's debate can be examined by modern day black intellectuals. West's (1993) book *Race Matters* asserted that the fundamental crisis in black America is twofold: too much poverty and too little self love. West suggests that the "quality of leadership is neither the product of one great individual nor the result of odd historical accidents. Rather, it comes from deeply bred traditions and communities that shape and mold talented and gifted persons" (p. 37). He noted that black political leaders are much more like Booker T. Washington when they confine themselves to the black turf, vowing to protect their leadership status and serving as power brokers with powerful non-blacks (usually white politicians). West described Du Bois as highly disciplined in life and intensely demanding. He stated that the crisis of black leadership can be remedied only if we candidly confront its existence.

The common denominator in this discussion of race and historical debate between Du Bois and Washington is that black people are viewed by white America as a "problem people." Du Bois's words echo in his 1903 classic *The Souls of Black Folk* in "Of Our Spiritual Strivings":

> They approach me in a half-hesitant sort of way, eye me curiously or compassionately, and then instead of saying directly, How does it feel to be a problem? [T]hey say, I know an excellent colored man in my town…Do not these Southern outrages make your blood boil? At these I smile, or am interested, or reduce the boiling to a simmer, as the occasion may require. To the real question, How does it feel to be a problem? I answer seldom a word. (p. 7)

Nearly a century later, West (1993) argued that we

have continued the discussion about race in America focusing on the "problems" black people pose for whites rather than examining what black people reveal about us as a nation (p. 3). This is another example of Du Bois's rare and unique intellectual insight.

Contemporary scholars (Gates & West, 1996, 2000; Lewis, 1993, 2000; West, 1993) discussed Du Bois and Washington's debate as being a clash of ideologies—stating that Du Bois was a radical intellectual and an idealist and describing Booker T. Washington as an accommodationist or a realist who accepted white dominance in order to achieve his goals. In their discussion of Washington and Du Bois, it was noted that the various strategies Du Bois advocated for the liberation of the Negro race often landed him on a collision course with Booker T. Washington and his supporters (Du Bois 1897, 1902, 1903, 1968a; Gates & West, 1996).

Frazier (1957) and Du Bois (1904) noted that the Negro Press, like the press of other ethnic and racial minorities in American life, was a medium for the expression of the opinions of the small intelligentsia among Negroes. Most of the Negro press, with the following few exceptions, supported Washington's programs. *Freedom's Journal* was established in 1827 by free Negroes, one of whom was John Russworm, the first Negro to graduate from an American college. The *North Star* by Frederick Douglass (a slave abolitionist and great orator) was concerned primarily with the abolition of slavery and with protest against civil discrimination against Negroes. The *Chicago Defender* was started in 1905, as a handbill, by Robert Abbott. His represented a departure from the traditional type of Negro paper that was designed to attract the attention of the Negro intelligentsia. The *Chicago Defender* attracted a more diverse and larger audience. *The Guardian*, published in Boston by Monroe Trotter (1905), a distinguished graduate of Harvard, expressed the militant demand of Negro intellectuals for Negro equality. The *New York Age* became the principal mouthpiece for the program of Booker T. Washington (Du Bois, 1903, 1904; Field, 1909; Frazier, 1957; Washington, 1901).

In the press, Washington (1895) constantly reassured Southern white leaders that progress could occur without threatening the established social order. Washington, at one time, offered Du Bois a position at Tuskegee. Du Bois turned it down because he became increasingly concerned over the dictatorial control Washington held over the black press, black political appointments, and black education. In *The Souls of Black Folk*, Du Bois's (1903a) critique is very much in the Frederick Douglass tradition of pushing for full civil, political and social rights.

This turn of the century debate between Washington and Du Bois is still with us at the beginning of the 21st century. It is commonly portrayed as a debate over the utility of economics, versus politics, as the best route to black advancement. Those who would argue that Booker T. Washington was right, in his emphasis on economic development, make a number of faulty assumptions. First, they assume that Du Bois won the debate, and that Washington's philosophy of "accommodation" was submerged. In fact, from 1895 until his death in 1915, Washington exercised more individual control over resources in the national black community than anyone before or since. However, toward the end of his life, Washington's grip was weakening due to the failure of accommodationism to produce results. "Jim Crow" and the lynchings of blacks continued unabated during his rein. Du Bois, on the other hand, had argued that the black person who succeeded economically is still at the mercy of whites because he or she has no power to protect his or her wealth without the vote (Logan, 1971).

Washington and Du Bois's debate was more fundamental than just the issue of the type of training that black people were to receive. It was a conflict of vision and values. For Washington, black culture represented an obstacle to advancement. His advocacy of social separatism was only a temporary strategy leading to assimilation. W. E. B. Du Bois, however, could not accept the dominant values of the day. He challenged the industrial education notion "that the world is simply bread and butter" (Du Bois,

1903). Moreover, he worried that material wants had developed much faster than social and moral standards (Du Bois, 1903, 1924; Logan, 1944).

Moon (1968, 1972) and Logan (1971) suggested that modern-day neoconservatives are just as fond of pointing out how out-of-step the leaders of civil rights organizations are as Washington's followers were in attacking Du Bois and the "Talented Tenth." Some have given the debate a more racial character by viewing Washington as a self-help separatist linked to Marcus Garvey and the Nation of Islam. J. H. Franklin (1972) and Lester (1971) view Du Bois as continuing an integrationist tradition established by Douglass and fully developed by Martin Luther King, Jr. Both views are simplistic and do more harm than good if we are to plan for the future based on an understanding of the past.

It is impossible to separate economic from political progress or vice-versa. Both Booker T. Washington and W. E. B. Du Bois recognized the relationship between economics and political power (Henry, 1992). However, Du Bois (1936) saw Washington as an opportunist. Du Bois also indicated that Washington believed in political rights for people who could exercise them, but in the case of southern Negroes, Washington followed the attitude of the white south, which was against political activity of any kind from black people. Du Bois (1903a) wrote that Washington's "work has wonderfully prospered, his friends are legion, and his enemies are confounded. To-day [sic] he stands as the one recognized spokesman of his ten million fellows, and one of the most notable figures in a nation of seventy millions [sic]" (Du Bois, 1903a, p. 40). However, it is here, also, that Du Bois first published his criticism of Booker T. Washington:

> And yet the time is come when one may speak in all sincerity and utter courtesy of the mistakes and shortcomings of Mr. Washington's career, as well as of his triumphs, without being thought captious or envious, and without forgetting that it is easier to do ill than well in the world. (Du Bois, 1903a, p. 40)

Du Bois's larger purpose was that of bringing to light the plight of African Americans after Washington's Atlanta Compromise. Du Bois believed Washington's philosophy represented, "in Negro thought the old attitude of adjustment and submission" (Du Bois, 1903a, p. 44) because it recommended foregoing political representation and civil rights training. Historically, Du Bois understood Washington's programs were to serve as a way for blacks to reach financial equality with whites, but he believed in the long run that the price was too high. In his chapter "Of Mr. Booker T. Washington and Others" in *The Souls of Black Folk*, Du Bois says:

> In the history of nearly all other races and

peoples the doctrine preached at such crises has been that manly self-respect is worth more than lands and houses, and that a people who voluntarily surrender such respect, or cease striving for it, are not worth civilizing (Du Bois, 1903a, p. 45).

Washington (1901, 1903) initiated the development of the Tuskegee Institute to help students learn skilled trades and perform them in an exceptional way. Manual training courses developed at Tuskegee served as models—not just in the United States but in nations all over the developing world. Presidents and dignitaries visited Tuskegee. Major philanthropic figures of the day supported it. John D. Rockefeller and Andrew Carnegie both contributed heavily to its operations.

African American critics charged that Tuskegee did little more than train its students to comply with the white social order of the South and that Tuskegee graduates, denied access to industrial positions, became domestic workers and manual laborers. However, Washington insisted that progress was being made (Andrews, 1985; Bennett, 1961).

Bond (1925) asserted that the chief value of industrial education is to give to the student habits of industry, thrift, economy and an idea of the dignity of labor. The economic condition of the African American people was inextricably linked to a lack of training and skills. Washington's aim was to provide avenues for American Negroes to improve their economic situation quickly by learning vocational skills and availing themselves of jobs in fields of manual labor. The debate was over much more than industrial/technical education versus liberal arts—or even economics versus politics. It was a debate over the fundamental character of American society. It was a conflict of values and vision (Davis, 1982; Du Bois, 1924).

❋ The Negro Academy

Throughout the course of my historical investigation into the life and works of W. E. B. Du Bois, I discovered, through the examination of both published and unpublished papers written by Du Bois and other scholars, that the seed of Du Bois's idea, articulated in the "Talented Tenth," was planted while he was a member of the Negro Academy and inspired by the suggestions of Alexander Crummell (Bell, 1996; Crummell, 1898; Du Bois, 1985; Huggins, 1986). Alexander Crummell, founder of the Negro Academy, was a friend and mentor to W. E. B. Du Bois. He played a pivotal role in the late nineteenth-century debates over race and the black intellectual (Bond, 1925; Clifford, 1903; Crummell, 1898; Du Bois, 1898;). Crummell was a strong force in Du Bois's intellectual life. They shared a common interest in self-help and the uplifting of the race (Ferris, 1913). The Negro

Academy was a forum for intellectual debate among various African American communities. Crummell often spoke out for black self-help, racial solidarity, and the advancement of African Americans. The American Negro Academy was organized to point out a practical path of advancement for the Negro people. It sought to gather talented, unselfish men and pure, noble-minded women.

In the 1898 *Encyclopedia of Africana* (the encyclopedia of the African American experience), the Negro Academy was noted as a learned society for African American men of letters, arts and sciences. Under the leadership of Alexander Crummell, scholars such as W. E. B. Du Bois, Carter G. Woodson and Alain Locke joined the Academy. The goals of the American Negro Academy (ANA) were to ensure recognition of African American advances in science, art, and literature. In addition, the organization sought to challenge and refute the circulation of racist and erroneous misinformation about African American life and culture. The ANA embodied Du Bois's later doctrine of the "Talented Tenth." This ideal, along with other philosophical differences regarding education, kept Booker T. Washington from ever being invited to join the ANA.

The Academy held its first general meeting on Friday, March 5, 1897. Eighteen of the most prominent African American men in the United States, including Du Bois, attended. The Presbyterian minister Francis J. Grimké read aloud Alexander Crummell's "Civilization, The Primal Need of the Race" (1898). It was the first of twenty-two occasional papers that were published during the nearly 31 years of the Academy's existence. In his paper, Crummell explained what he saw as the Academy's "special undertaking": the cultural work of uplifting black people onto the "grand plane of civilization." This goal was to be achieved by the scientific processes of literature, art, and philosophy and through the agency of the cultured men of this same Negro race (Du Bois, 1911).

Like many of the men who associated with him, Crummell defined culture in terms of a group's highest achievements in the arts, literature, and scholarship. This emphasis on high culture was intended to rebuke nearly two centuries of claims—by white, particularly European, scholars and intellectuals—that black people were inherently incapable of producing anything of substance in the realm of artistic and intellectual activity.

According to Du Bois's (1969) occasional paper of the Negro Academy, "The Conservation of Races," men of Science, Letters, and Arts, or those distinguished in other walks of life, sought to ensure that only the most thoughtful men were charged with the task of representing, to the black masses and to the white world, the highest achievements of the growing black intelligentsia. The stakes were high that day for the men assembled at the Lincoln Memorial Church in Washington, D.C.

The American Negro Academy's activities included conferences, meetings, research, data collection, and youth outreach. Between 1897 and 1924, twenty-two occasional papers were presented at Academy meetings, disseminating the thinking of leading African American intellectuals on a wide range of issues. Academy members were instrumental in the formation of similar activities and organizations throughout the country.

In creating the American Negro Academy, Alexander Crummell sought to avoid opportunistic black men who, instead of fighting for the race, would do the bidding of whites in exchange for fame and fortune (Du Bois, 1898). There were nine original organizers of the Academy: four ministers, three professors, one publisher and one poet—including the young Du Bois, who was then in Philadelphia working at the University of Pennsylvania on his classic work *The Philadelphia Negro* (Du Bois, 1899).

The Negro Academy sought to gather noble minded, cultured, and unselfish men and women whose aim was to be the epitome of the black intellectual in America, to be representative in character, impartial in conduct, and firm in leadership (Crummell, 1898; Du Bois, 1903, 1925; Paschal, 1971). Alexander Crummell was elected its first president.

According to Byerman (1994), Quarles (1969), and Asante (1988, 1991), the Academy's first goal was to promote the recognition of contributions by people of African ancestry to the fields of literature, history, science, art and other areas of the humanities. The group believed that within each race, the most intellectually endowed should lead the masses toward the goals and subsequent rewards of civilization. That philosophy was reiterated by Du Bois as his concept of leadership: a select group of college educated Negro intellectuals with a commitment to service, which would be called the Talented Tenth.

Activities of the Negro Academy, until 1924, consisted of publishing occasional papers by its scholars, hosting annual meetings, supporting research, and offering programs to raise the intellectual aspirations and achievements of youths. The Academy was an advocate of research centers to ensure that the African experience would be studied. The Academy's scholarly writings reflected its concern with challenging and refuting racist research that disparaged African Americans' contributions to world civilization (Moss, 1981).

Aptheker (1948, 1966) noted that many of the individuals involved in the Academy branched off into activities not directly organized by Crummell's group. For example, Du Bois, while a professor at Atlanta University, organized a series of meetings during 1905-1906 called The Conference of the

Negro Problem. Alain Locke coordinated the work of writers and artists during the 1920s who became part of the Harlem Renaissance. John Hope pioneered educational reform as president of Morehouse College. James Weldon Johnson made his mark in the literary field, as well as in civil rights and international affairs.

In the early decades of the twentieth century, the Academy laid the groundwork for subsequent organizations such as Carter G. Woodson's Association of the Study of Afro-American Life and History. And Crummell's own interests and experiences in the West African country of Liberia were widely recognized. (Moss, 1981).

Crummell (1898) encouraged Du Bois to write his leadership proposal of the "Talented Tenth." He perceived Du Bois to be the ideal black man: communicative, cultured, intense, and sensitive to the moral significance of race. Crummell, likewise, stood for all the things Du Bois valued: education, integrity, hard work, sacrifice, and perseverance. Crummell was the hero of Du Bois's double consciousness: asserting his racial identity but seeking to raise his race through the faith of the Episcopal Church.

According to Byerman (1994) and V. P. Franklin (1995), Crummell and Du Bois drew a contrast between men's physical needs and the needs of their souls. Crummell and Du Bois viewed Booker T. Washington, with his movement of industrial education for the black masses, as a sell-out to white America, and they forcefully challenged the Tuskegee principles of industrial education for blacks. They saw Booker T. Washington's program for blacks as one of accommodation to the status quo. They believed that instead of encouraging higher education for black youths, Washington encouraged learning vocational skills and seeking approval from white America. The philosophical differences between Du Bois and Washington led to what we have come to know as a historical debate: the training of hands versus the training of brains.

For about fifteen years after its inception, the Negro Academy managed to sustain itself with membership fees and to produce a few papers that are now considered classic examples of late nineteenth and early twentieth century African American scholarship. Among them are Kelly Miller's "A Review of Hoffman's Race Traits and Tendencies of the American Negro" (1897), W. E. B. Du Bois's "The Conservation of Races" (1897), Archibald H. Grimké's "Right on the Scaffold, or the Martyrs of 1822" (1901), William S. Scarborough's "The Educated Negro and His Mission" (1903), and William H. Ferris's "Alexander Crummell, an Apostle of Negro Culture" (1920).

However, the Academy's broader goal of establishing itself as a major intellectual presence was never realized. The burgeoning black masses, on whose behalf the Academy claimed to be working, were much too engaged with merely surviving to be impressed with the lofty ideals of a few highly educated black men. Particularly after World War I, black men returning from European battlegrounds expecting to reap the rewards of full citizenship found, instead, that America's racial barriers had been made even more impenetrable. The idea that a black learned society would open the way for black cultural redemption was unfathomable (Ellison, 1952).

❈ Prelude to the Niagara Movement

Dorothy Drinkard-Hawkshawe (1977), noted that the National Federation of Colored Men of the United States was a prelude to both the Niagara Movement and the National Association for the Advancement of Colored People (NAACP). This group of black men was organized in December of 1895. It was the outcome of a conference that was called by John H. Jones, a Chicago attorney, George L. Know, W. Allison Sween, attorney from Indianapolis, and E. H. Morris of Chicago. Many black citizens attended to discuss their "condition" and "the principles and measures important to the welfare, progress and general improvement of the race." (Du Bois, 1905, p. 70).

The Federation's president was David Augustus Straker, a native-born Barbadian who had established an illustrious career as a lawyer, educator, lecturer, and newspaper publisher. Drinkard-Hawkshawe

(1977) noted that Straker spent the rest of his life in the struggle to win human equality. His work with the National Federation of Colored Men of the United States was a very important part of that struggle. "As president of the organization, Straker pleaded for cooperation throughout the United States so that, through united efforts, blacks could cast off their 'load of oppression' and 'dispel an unjust, unfounded and cruel hate'" (p. 53). The intention of this group was to establish subordinate organizations to carry on the work of the parent body. In order to achieve this end, the organization divided the United States into districts.

The specific objectives of the Federation were remarkably similar to those of the Niagara Movement, which was convened in 1905, and to those of the NAACP, which was organized in 1909. Straker asserted that he was not opposed to industrial training, as proposed by Booker T. Washington, but was a greater advocate for employment more related to educational opportunities. He felt that education was necessary for black economic and social progress and also for fostering an awareness of the duties and responsibilities of citizenship. The Federation demanded that certain provisions of the United States be enforced, notably the sixth amendment, which granted the right to a speedy and public trial by an impartial jury; and the fourteenth and fifteenth amendments, which provide due process of law, the equal protection of the law, and the right to vote (Drinkard-Hawkshawe, 1977).

Straker expressed the position of the Federation clearly, "We view with alarm the recent decision of the Supreme Court of the United States...in which the unjust and nefarious method of discriminating among passengers traveling in steamcars, within several of the Southern states...has been upheld by law, and we are determined to no longer be discriminated against, as American citizens" (Drinkard-Hawkshawe, 1977, pp. 53-54). The Federation proposed to achieve its objectives through political pressure and agitation.

Drinkard-Hawkshawe (1977) tells of the demise of the Federation and the beginnings of the Niagara movement:

> Ten years after the organization of the Federation, another movement, of which Straker was a part, was organized. The new effort to achieve black unity was known as the Niagara Movement. It was officially launched in July, 1905, following an earlier preliminary conference which was described in a letter dated January 13, 1905, to W. E. B. Du Bois:
>
>> At [a] conference held at Mr. Trotter's office today it was agreed that a committee of representative men should visit the President and present broad lines of policy which we desire him to pursue concerning the colored race.

> Three definite propositions have been suggested:
>
> First: That the Facilities of the Attorney General's office be utilized to uphold the Fifteenth Amendment in connection with cases that may be brought in the Supreme Court, testing the constitutionality of the revised Constitutions of the South. [This was in reference to the Grandfather Clauses].
>
> Second: To wield the influence of the administration to carry out the Interstate Commerce Clause of the Constitution affecting interstate traffic including the passenger service.
>
> Third: To encourage national aid to education in the most needy states. (Drinkard-Hawkshawe, 1977, p. 56)

❋ The Niagara Movement

Du Bois and twenty-nine black intellectuals, from seventeen states in America, held their inaugural meeting on the Canadian side of Niagara Falls in 1905. Du Bois had originally intended the group to meet in Buffalo, New York and had written to reserve rooms at one of the hotels there. However, "Race prejudice on the part of the Buffalo hotel establishment had forced the conference organizer to rush to Fort Erie [in Ontario, Canada] on the evening of the ninth to arrange alternate accommodations" (Lewis, 1993, pp. 316-317). The racism of the managers of the Buffalo hotel illustrated the importance of the purpose behind the Niagara Movement. Lewis says it well, "There was irony in the fact that the first collective attempt by African-Americans to demand full citizenship rights in the twentieth century (without even indirect support of influential whites) had been forced to spring to life on Canadian soil" (p. 317).

This meeting gave birth to the Niagara Movement, which was incorporated in the District of Columbia on January 31, 1906. The Niagara Movement received its name from Niagara Falls and met annually in Niagara Falls, Canada. Their reason for meeting in Canada was due to the racism that existed in the United States—the denial of access to public education, accommodations, and voting rights. The group called for the use of protest and agitation as strategies for bringing about change and better conditions for African Americans (Du Bois, 1905; Ferris 1913).

Booker T. Washington disagreed with the group's methods and intent, and consequently, he exerted his negative political influence. Du Bois had asked only, "a few selected persons" (Rudwick, 1957, p. 177) to the Niagara meetings. However, Ralph Bunche reported (as cited in Rudwick, 1957), that many of those invited, "declined at the last minute after being pressured by white friends of Booker T. Washington"

(Rudwick, 1957, p. 177). Washington denied that race prejudice was increasing and repudiated the anti-segregation stand of the Niagara men (Du Bois, 1905).

Rudwick (1957) states that Du Bois was elected as the first General Secretary of the Niagara Movement. By this time, Du Bois was recognized "as the second most prominent living Negro...and Negro college graduates especially considered him the representative of the race's aspiration" (Rudwick, 1957, p. 177).

Aptheker (1948, 1973) described the men involved with the Niagara Movement as anti-Tuskegee. Bunche (1913) and Du Bois (1908) noted that no African American voice had been heard with such great authority as that of Booker T. Washington, and the militant Niagara Movement was a direct response to Washington's cautious approach to racial justice. It was an important step in the formation of modern African American protest.

Du Bois (1905) stated that the Niagara Movement evolved from his concept of the Talented Tenth, and he demanded recognition of black leadership in the United States, pursuant to the laws of the Constitution. Members of the Niagara Movement were to meet with President Theodore Roosevelt, but the meeting never took place. Aptheker (1948) suggests that the meeting with President Roosevelt was cancelled because Roosevelt's own position was more in favor of Washington's ideas than those of Du Bois. Du Bois was considered a controversial political agitator advocating racial equality. He was too critical of white America. Under the advisement of his administration, President Roosevelt postponed the meeting (Aptheker, 1948).

Rudwick (1960) noted, in his assessment of the Niagara Movement, that Du Bois's intemperate statements made the Niagara Movement especially vulnerable. Du Bois (1968a) admitted that the Niagara Movement suffered because of the strain between his own dynamic personality and that of Monroe Trotter (a member of the Talented Tenth). The Washingtonians, meanwhile, often asserted that Du Bois's excesses were representative of the entire association, and that the Talented Tenth were not "leaders" of the race. Andrews (1985) indicated, similarly, that the Talented Tenth was an ostensibly arrogant group, which lent credence to the accusations of Du Bois's moral elitism.

Despite all of these limitations and oppositions, the members of the Niagara Movement could be justifiably proud of their efforts on behalf of higher education for Negro youths, their contributions to legal redress for civil rights violations, and their attempt to organize a political lobby composed of informed, independent, and articulate citizens. As exponents of the strategy of protest, they provided an alternative to Washington's accommodation.

Most of the scholars who researched and wrote

about the Talented Tenth discussed the Niagara Movement as a guide that influenced public opinion. In *The Autobiography of W. E. B. Du Bois: A Soliloquy on Viewing My Life from the Last Decade of Its First Century* (Du Bois, 1968a), Du Bois stated that his leadership of the Niagara Movement was based on writing and teaching, whereas Washington's leadership had become a matter of money and political power, which Du Bois called the "Tuskegee Machine." The "Tuskegee Machine," backed by white capital, worked against Du Bois and the black intellectual.

Lester (1971) was one who saw the Niagara Movement as an example of the struggle for manhood, suffrage, and abolition of caste distinctions based on race, color, and gender. It was founded upon a belief in the dignity of labor, along with the principle that the highest and best education and training is a monopoly of no class or race. The Niagara Movement united efforts to realize these ideas under wise and courageous leadership. In the final analysis, the Talented Tenth was seeking remedies for the Jim Crow laws (Du Bois, 1905, 1968a).

In arguing for the need for the Niagara Movement to evolve into a more formal organization, Du Bois (1905) wrote, "The first explanation of any hearing of this new movement will naturally be: 'Another!' Why, we may legitimately be asked, should men attempt another organization after failures of the past? We answer soberly but earnestly, 'for that very reason'"

(p. 150). According to Du Bois (1905), the Niagara Movement was created to end the curtailment of political rights, achieve civil rights, organize business cooperation, urge Negroes to vote, and build school houses to increase the interest in education. They also sought to open up new avenues of employment, distribute information on health, bring Negroes and labor unions into mutual understanding, and to study Negro history. The Niagara movement would do this through the circulation of honest, unsubsidized newspapers and periodicals. Ultimately, it meant doing whatever was necessary to claim their manhood in the performance of their duties.

Rudwick (1957), in the *Journal of Negro History*, reported at length on the manifesto of that first historic meeting of the Niagara Movement:

> The platform of the 1905 Niagara sessions was written in vigorous and sharp tones. The conferees placed the responsibility for the Negro problem squarely on the shoulders of the whites. The radicals were not asking for opinions; they were making definite demands:
> 1. Freedom of speech and criticism—[t]he fluid exchange of ideas was crucial to the Talented Tenth...
> 2. An unfettered and unsubsidized press...
> 3. Manhood suffrage—[t]he conferees desired to participate in the American political system (North and South) on the

same basis as the whites...
4. The abolition of all caste distinctions based simply on race and color...
5. The recognition of the principles of human brotherhood as a practical present creed...
6. Recognition of the highest and best human training as a monopoly of no class or race...
7. A belief in the dignity of labor...
8. United effort to realize these ideals under wise and courageous leadership. (Rudwick, 1957, pp. 178-179)

The Niagara Movement developed a hard core of uncompromising Negroes who matched in intensity the unyielding Washingtonians, and during this battle, the Negro race may not have profited very much in the short run. Nevertheless, the Niagara men (and their friends in other equal rights organizations) put forth a set of blueprints which were to be the guidelines for many Negroes and whites and held several important conferences in Niagara, Harpers Ferry, and Boston. Gradually, Washington receded in influence, while Du Bois and the Niagara Movement were vindicated after the NAACP appeared on the scene (Bond, 1925; Henry, 1992; Rudwick, 1960).

In 1910, W. E. B. Du Bois and a few members of the Talented Tenth merged with an organization that had been initiated by Mary White Ovington, a social worker, and cofounded the National Association for the Advancement of Colored People (NAACP).

❋ The National Association for the Advancement of Colored People (NAACP)

The history of the NAACP dates back to June 1, 1909. This was the day of the interracial conference held at Henry Street Settlement in New York. From that conference emerged the National Negro Committee with an initial membership of 40. Du Bois and core members of the remnants of the Niagara Movement were its cofounders. In May 1910, during the second annual meeting of the National Negro Committee, the members decided to change the name to the National Association for the Advancement of Colored People (NAACP). It was incorporated under the laws of New York.

The following were people who held pioneering executive positions for the NAACP: Mr. Moorfield Storey, a lawyer in Boston; William English Walling, Chairman of the executive committee; John Milholland, the treasurer; Frances Blascoer, Executive Secretary; and W. E. B. Du Bois, Director of Publicity and Research. Being bi-racial and national in scope, the NAACP went beyond the boundaries of religion, politics, social, and class lines in uniting African Americans to fight for their rights. It employed peaceful methods of persuasion such as the press, the petition, ballots, and court proceedings to push for its demands. The NAACP (1910) defined itself as "an organization to end racial discrimination and segregation in all public aspects of American life."

Thus, out of the impulse of the Niagara Movement, the NAACP was formed, and in November 1910, *The Crisis* first appeared as its house publication. The first Annual Report issued in January 1911 gives the purpose of the NAACP:

> The National Association for the Advancement of Colored People seeks to uplift the colored men and women of this country by securing to them the full enjoyment of their rights as citizens, justice in all courts, and equality of opportunity everywhere. It favors, and aims to aid, every kind of education among them save that which teaches special privileges or prerogative, class or caste. It recognizes the national character of the Negro problem and no sectionalism. It believes in the holding of the Constitution of the United States and its Amendments, in the spirit of Abraham Lincoln. It upholds the doctrine of "all men up and no man down." It abhors Negro crime, but still more the conditions which breed crime, and most of all the crimes committed by mobs in the mockery of the law, or by individuals in the name of the law.
>
> It believes that the scientific truths of the

Negro problem must be available before the country can see its way wholly clear to right existing wrongs. It has no other beliefs than that the best way to uplift the colored man and best way to aid the white man to peace is social content; it has no other desire than exacting justice, and no other motive than patriotism. (NAACP First Annual Report, January 1, 1911)

The work of the NAACP in the succeeding 92 years is well known. Its greatest triumph has been in the field of legal defense of Negroes and Negro rights. With the help of the foremost legal talent of the nation, it has secured from the U. S. Supreme Court decisions which in principle establish:

1. Recognition of the validity of the Fifteenth Amendment.
2. The unconstitutionality of residential segregation laws and ordinances.
3. The unconstitutionality of the "Grandfather" clauses in Southern State constitutions.
4. The right of Negroes to sit on juries.
5. The dictum that "due process of law" may be violated by the threat of mob violence.
6. The denial of the right of the state to segregate primary elections race. (Du Bois, 1985)

In addition, scores of individuals have been

defended, and the most effective and sustained anti-lynching campaign in the history of the country has been carried out—though not yet to the successful passage of a Federal anti-lynching law.

Though the NAACP began through philanthropic aid from wealthy white liberals, it became in its best years more and more of a Negro supported effort (Du Bois, 1968a). From 1912 to 1927, Negroes were making substantial advancements along economic lines. It is no accident that a Negro organization, especially for self-improvement and defense, was at its peak during that period. By 1928, the economic progress of the Negro had begun to slow down. From 1910 until the Depression, the NAACP was the most effective militant organization in Negro life, and its success was unquestioned.

In Du Bois's (1968a) autobiography, *A Soliloquy on Viewing My Life from the Last Decade of its First Century*, he wrote a notable account of the NAACP's activities. The NAACP started within one hundred years of the birth of Abraham Lincoln. The city of Springfield, Illinois had a longtime white southern resident, William English Walling, who dramatized a terribly gruesome event. This portrayal prompted a group of liberals to form a committee in New York, which Du Bois was invited to attend. A conference sponsored by the same committee was held in 1909. Du Bois accepted the offer to become a member of their organization in 1910, in New York, as its Director of Publications and Research. In August of 1910, Du Bois left the south and reported to his new office in New York, at 20 Vesey Street.

The NAACP was designed to be a program for change. After its formation in 1910, the NAACP very quickly clarified its task. It would concern itself with the problem of achieving first class citizenship for black people rather than becoming bogged down in questions of social equality. Because it worked primarily in the area of legal rights, the NAACP never really became an organization of the black masses. There is no question, however, of the importance of this legal rights struggle, which underscored the notion, during Du Bois's time as in the present, that the United States Constitution is only as good as its enforcement (Frazier, 1971).

The NAACP developed and adopted a document toward the end of its first decade of existence. This policy, *The Task for the Future—A Program for 1919*, has remained virtually unchanged to this present day. It was printed in *The Crisis* in 1919, listing nine objectives with which to strengthen the Association's organization and resources. Its chief aim has been restated many times:

1. A vote for every Negro on the same terms as for white men and women.
2. An equal chance to acquire the same kind of education that will enable the Negro everywhere wisely to use this vote.

3. A fair trial, in courts for all crimes of which he is accused, by judges in whose election he has participated without discrimination because of race.
4. A right to sit on the jury, which passes judgment upon him.
5. Defense against lynchings and burning at the hands of mobs.
6. Equal service on railroads and public carriers: to include sleeping car service, dining car service, and pullman service at the same cost and upon the same terms as other passengers.
7. Equal rights to the use of public parks, libraries, and other community services for which he is taxed.
8. An equal chance for a livelihood in public and private employment.
9. The abolition of color-hyphenation and the substitution of "straight Americanism." (Broderick, 1959; Du Bois, 1919, 1968a; Rudwick, 1960)

Such a fight was outlined as worthy of the support of all Americans and printed in an unstructured and disjointed treatment by Langston Hughes and Du Bois and in a collection of essays called "Race Adjustment" by Kelly Miller (1909).

The NAACP called upon believers in democracy to join them in a national conference for the discussion of present evils, the voicing of protests, and the renewal of the struggle for civil and political liberty. According to Du Bois (1915, 1920), his role was to secure financial support for the Association and to encourage individuals to join. Many of the Talented Tenth brought their energies and abilities into the service of the Association, and it grew as a result. The NAACP currently has over 500,000 members, 1,700 branch chapters, and 450 college and youth chapters (Jackson, 1997).

A report in *Jet Magazine* (February 27, 1995; p. 19) claimed that men and women in the NAACP struggled with organizational and ideological problems since the first major expansion sixty years ago. The stunning success of the NAACP was its legal campaign and the spin-off of the Legal Defense Fund. More than gesture was needed, and the organization moved quickly to re-examine its basic premise.

By the 1930s, Du Bois felt strongly that the basic policies and direction of the NAACP needed to be revisited (Du Bois, 1931). Earlier, he wrote that the Talented Tenth share an "inner Negro cultural ideal" based upon ancient African Communism, supported and developed by the memory of slavery and the experience of caste. This drove the Negro group into a spiritual unity precluding the development of economic classes and inner class struggles (Du Bois, 1920). During August 18-21, 1933, a second summit was held to engage young intellectuals in problem solving strategies. However, they were criticized by the Urban League for placing too much emphasis on the Talented Tenth and not enough on the suffering masses. This was Du Bois's dominant ideological perspective while he worked at Atlanta University and during his years at *The Crisis*, but by the late 1950s, many members of the Talented Tenth appeared to be betraying that ideal or acting as if it did not exist. Du Bois (1968a) stated:

> We must admit that the majority of the American Negro intelligentsia, together with much of the West Indian and West African leadership shows symptoms of following in the footsteps of western acquisitive society, with its exploitation of labor, monopoly of land and its resources, and with private profit for the privileged in a world of poverty, disease, ignorance, as the natural end of human culture. (p. 262)

Du Bois could not understand a world of incessant lynchings and segregation against blacks in the face of modern civilization of the early twentieth century. As a young man of 37, Du Bois became a militant in the interest of his race (Du Bois, 1909, 1910). He recognized the utility of an association or an organ by which he could fight for civil rights in the United States of America. *The Crisis* served as a vehicle through which the voice of black Americans could express their dissatisfaction with white America, and be heard, which was a dangerous and delicate matter (Bennett, 1994; Du Bois, 1968a).

The Crisis was impaired by Du Bois's lack of training in business management. He was his own manager, which meant a loss of much time to details. Then there was the matter of policy; of how far he should go in expressing his own ideas and reactions. Du Bois argued that no organization could express definite opinions. The NAACP came to its conclusions and stated them in its annual resolutions; whereas *The Crisis* stated openly the opinion of its editor (Du Bois), as long as the opinion was in general agreement with the organization. Du Bois (1968a) indicated that this was a dangerous and delicate matter and would eventually break down when there was considerable divergence of opinion between the editor and the organization. Indeed, difference of opinion on the majority of policies led to the dissolution of this interesting partnership.

One of the first difficulties that the association had to work out was the case of its attitude toward Booker T. Washington. Being conscious of the inevitable conflict, Du Bois (1968a) intended, from the very beginning, to be careful in his attempt to avoid any exaggeration of their differences of thought. However, in order for Du Bois to discuss the Negro question in 1910, he had to discuss Booker T. Washington, who, while in London, had "assured the distinguished members of the Anti-Slavery and

Aborigines Protection Society that the American race problem was virtually solved" (Lewis, 1993, p. 414). Through the mechanism of *The Crisis,* Du Bois openly challenged Washington's conciliatory report. Du Bois's militancy not only took the form of writing and editing, but also that of organizing. Du Bois helped organize the Races Conference in London in 1911. The purpose of the Congress was to bring together representatives of numerous ethnic and cultural groups and also to bring new and honest conceptions of scientific basis of racial and social relations of people. Du Bois (1968a) indicated that he had the opportunity to address the Congress twice within the hall of the University of London and to write one of the two poems which greeted the assembly.

Returning to the United States, Du Bois plunged into a campaign in which he saw a chance to develop a third party movement on a broad platform of votes for Negroes and industrial democracy. Du Bois (1968a) wrote the proposed party platform:

> The Progressive party recognizes that distinctions of race or class in political life have no place in a democracy. Especially does the party realize that a group of 10,000,000 people who have in a generation changed from a slave to a free labor system, reestablished family life, accumulated $1,000,000,000 of real property, including 20,000,000 acres

of land, and reduced their illiteracy from 80 to 30 percent, deserve and must have justice, opportunity and a voice in their own government. (p. 263)

Members of the NAACP advocated and worked in vain for the adoption of the third party movement. However, Du Bois (1968a) stated that President "Theodore Roosevelt would have none of it" (p. 263). He told Mr. Joel V. Spingarn (co-founder of the NAACP) that he should be "careful of that man Du Bois," who was in Roosevelt's opinion a "dangerous person" (Du Bois, 1968a, p. 263). Du Bois was angered by Roosevelt's comment and, therefore, utilized his editorial skills in *The Crisis* against Roosevelt for re-election as president. He spoke favorably of Woodrow Wilson, who eventually repudiated his promise of support for the Negroes and supported instead new discriminatory bills both in Congress and among the states.

According to Du Bois (1968a), the NAACP was cast in a difficult position as "[t]he socialists began to consider the color line and to discriminate against the membership of colored people in the South, lest whites should not be attracted" (p. 264) to their movement. The NAACP tried to get the President to appoint a National Race Commission, but nothing was done. Then, war hit the world: the Chinese Revolution in 1912; the Balkan War in 1912-13; and, ultimately, the First World War.

In that same year, the NAACP sponsored Mr. Spingarn and Du Bois to attend a meeting of the National Council of Social Agencies in Memphis, Tennessee, advertising the color question, "for all who dared to hear the truth" (Du Bois, 1968a, p. 265). Their success and later that year, the death of Booker T. Washington led to the first Amenia Conference—an effort to unite the American Negro into one movement. Finally, the World War touched America. With it came a sudden increase of lynchings and other brutal and inhumane acts of violence against Negroes and renewed segregation. The NAACP offered their services to fight. Then came the ultimate question, "Why should you fight for this country?" (Du Bois, 1968a, p. 265). The NAACP began recording the casualties of war, and documenting the numbers of black and white soldiers.

In addition to Du Bois's continuous work with the NAACP, and editing *The Crisis,* he worked tirelessly to develop Negro art and literature and fight the battle of liberalism against race prejudice. He tried to relate the war and post war problem to the question of racial justice. He attempted to show from the injustices of war time what the new vision must encompass. He watched and explained the political situations and traveled and lectured over thousands of miles and in hundreds of centers.

Simultaneous to his work at the NAACP, Du Bois published: *Darkwater* in 1920; *The Gift of Black Folk* in 1924; an essay on Georgia in *These United States* in 1924. Du Bois also wrote the concluding chapter in *The New Negro* edited by Alain Locke in 1925. As part of his transformational leadership, he mentored young intellectuals and supported most of the young writers who began what was called the "Renaissance of Negro Literature" in the 1920s, by publishing their voices in *The Crisis* magazine.

Having decided during the 1920s that the NAACP was on the wrong track, Du Bois began to disagree with the civil libertarian texture of the Niagara-NAACP idea. In 1934, Du Bois declared open war on the NAACP in a series of articles in *The Crisis* stating that Negroes must use segregation to smash segregation by organizing producer and consumer cooperatives and cultivating the political, economic, and cultural strength of black Americans.

The ruling elite of the NAACP was horrified. Other NAACP leaders repudiated Du Bois's views in *The Crisis*, and Du Bois repudiated them in *The Crisis*. The controversy became extremely bitter and public, and as a result, Du Bois resigned and returned to Atlanta University. But the Pandora's box he had opened could not be easily closed.

Racism was, in fact, increasing, and the economic position of black Americans was deteriorating. The NAACP was virtually the de facto government of black America, and the foundation had been laid for the gains and problems of today. (Bennett,

1994; Huggins, 1986; Logan, 1971). To understand the gains and problems, we have to go back to that tumultuous time, in the spirit of Ralph Ellison, who once said, "the end is in the beginning and lies far ahead" (Ellison, 1947/1995, p. 6).

Kellogg (1967) wrote that dissension within the organization caused a great deal of trouble for the new association. Much mistrust among the members themselves began to surface. Female members Ida B. Wells and Mary Ovington, both chartered members of the NAACP, began to voice their displeasure about the patronizing and controlling attitudes of the male academics and about Du Bois's conflicts of interest with other agencies. Jealousy invaded the NAACP, with each member seeking his or her own place in the limelight.

Friction in the national office continued. Du Bois was accused by a few of the NAACP members of insolence and impertinence. According to the Villard to Garrison correspondence (1913), the Du Bois to Villard correspondence (1913), and the NAACP's board minutes (1913) further trouble with *The Crisis* and NAACP officers precipitated more resignations from members. Du Bois, however, remained defiant and insubordinate in regard to *The Crisis* and was accused of refusing to recognize the paper as an organ of the NAACP. The NAACP, however, reluctantly continued to put up with Du Bois's independence because he was a prominent, if annoying, member.

The NAACP board minutes of December 2, 1913 noted that the board did not accept any of Du Bois's proposals. This was their first step in countering his moves in *The Crisis*. Under the aegis of the association, they adopted a resolution that each issue of the magazine should clearly and prominently state the aims and objectives of the NAACP and the duty of *Crisis* readers to become members. This was followed by steps to copyright *The Crisis*, and its contents, in the name of the NAACP. In an attempt to overcome these problems, the NAACP's board hammered out a new policy throughout the spring and summer along with a new constitution and bylaws drawn up and approved by the Board.

Du Bois continued to wield much influence over the membership. However, his impolitic and sometimes arrogant behavior placed him under constant scrutiny and garnered a strong desire by the board to get rid of him. Du Bois (1914) blamed the NAACP's internal conflict on the color line, which the NAACP board members vehemently denied. In October 1919, Spingarn asked to be released from his position as chairman because he saw no end to Du Bois's "disruptive" role in the NAACP (Du Bois, 1920; Lewis, 1993).

Du Bois's (1940) activities increased. He became involved in West Africa, in an effort to help liberate Africa. Stewart (1984), Green (1977), and Watson (1934) suggested that out of necessity, Du Bois turned to separate economic issues and black nationalism. In turning toward a self-help program of economic organization along racial lines, Du Bois came into open conflict with his colleagues on the NAACP board of directors. The latter considered that by launching such a program, Du Bois was opposing the goals of the NAACP and was undermining its struggle for racial integration.

Du Bois (1915, 1940) argued, rather, that it was high time for the NAACP to change the direction of its struggle for Negro freedom. Social reforms through the Legal Defense Fund, with the financial support of black and white philanthropy, had revealed its limitations and its inability to reach the objectives of the association in its struggle against segregation.

In spite of his continued defense of the NAACP against communist slander, Du Bois admitted that "the platform of the NAACP is no complete program of social reform. It is a pragmatic union of certain definite problems while far beyond its program lies the whole question of the future of the darker races and economic emancipation of the working classes." (Du Bois, 1968a, p. 232). The pressing major question that must be faced by both the NAACP and the black population was, "How shall American Negroes be emancipated from economic slavery?" (Du Bois, 1968a, p. 233).

The rupture between Du Bois and NAACP Board of Directors occurred in 1934 with the resignation of

Du Bois from the Board and as Editor of *The Crisis*. It has been generally interpreted by both Du Bois, and most of his biographers and commentators, as a rupture between black nationalism and white liberalism (Aptheker, 1951; Brody, 1972; Du Bois, 1934). In 1943, he served on the Council of African Affairs, which raised a furor among the executives of the NAACP and led to Du Bois's final dismissal from the organization.

The point of Du Bois's program of cooperative economics was that the economic power to be acquired by African American people, through internal solidarity, should be geared toward social ends. Although Du Bois's program was very different from the one advocated by Booker T. Washington (1903), the social ends were the same (to have blacks uplift their quality of life by improving their economic condition). The goal of Du Bois's program was to create more social services within the black community, in order to increase the standards of living for all members of the community and not just some individuals (Du Bois, 1939; Logan, 1944).

Du Bois (1923) and Bond (1980) stated that, on the other hand, if the Negro is to develop his or her own power and gifts, if he or she is to fight prejudices and oppression successfully, all must unite for ideas higher than the world has ever realized. Especially in art, industry, and social change-building a new and great Negro ethos. Du Bois (1940, 1944, 1950) realized that even if political and economic equality of blacks were achieved, still, social integration of African American people would not take place unless the racial factor ceased to determine social interactions of American people with one another.

After drawing a distinction between race and culture, Moses (1978, 1992) points out that, racism, not cultural differences, prevented black inclusion in full citizenship. Moses's own experience, as an African American Catholic youth in the 1950s in Detroit, taught him about cultural relativism in American society.

❋ Summary

Chapter two emphasized Du Bois's leadership in its early stages. Du Bois's leadership ideas were inspired by Alexander Crummell, founder of the Negro Academy, who is credited with organizing the black intelligentsia. Crummell, a scholar, minister, and black intellectual, was deeply admired by Du Bois. He symbolized everything Du Bois hoped to become, and he opposed Booker T. Washington's self-proclaimed leadership of the black community. Du Bois was challenged by the Negro Academy, and by Crummell, to become a race leader. He accepted the call to uplift his people and advocated higher education and community service. Du Bois's leadership proposal, and his tireless pursuit of truth and excellence, were developed to deal with and attempt to resolve, the Negro's problems. Du Bois sought to develop and train college educated youths: his Talented Tenth. He urged the Talented Tenth to prioritize their lives, join his leadership program, and not compromise themselves for material or capital gain.

Du Bois's first attempt to mobilize the Talented Tenth was through the Niagara Movement, which he founded in 1905 in an effort to counteract Washington's theory of Industrialism. However, the Niagara Movement was short-lived. Du Bois was unsuccessful in gaining the financial and political support that Washington had achieved. Washington's leadership was less threatening to white America, whereas Du Bois's leadership was perceived as being too radical and agitating.

The twenty-nine members of the Talented Tenth held their meetings in Niagara Falls, Canada, because there they felt respected for their character as opposed to being disrespected because of their race.

Du Bois asserted that Washington's position would produce a defenseless, ignorant mass of people by enticing them to focus on becoming property owners and businessmen. Du Bois recognized these as restricted franchises that promoted segregation and limited training. Washington's program supported common schools and industrial trade and opposed higher education. It encouraged black America to "cast down" their buckets and be accepted through hard work in seeking the accumulation of wealth. Du Bois asserted that this was utterly paradoxical and submissive to racism and would produce a defenseless population without the rights of suffrage. Du Bois extended the philosophical debate with Washington arguing that Washington depreciated institutions of higher learning.

Du Bois (1939, 1968, 1982) voiced his disappointment in the future of the Talented Tenth and was prompted to reassess his own leadership idea, because of what the Talented Tenth had become. He (Du Bois, 1939, 1968a) blamed the failure of the concept of the "Talented Tenth" on greed, selfishness, capitalistic, and materialistic values, which he felt replaced the values of service and hard work. In his 1968 autobiography, he (Du Bois, 1968a) stated that he had believed that the men of the Talented Tenth could guide America into a higher level of civilization. But he acknowledged that many well-educated blacks had somehow become exploiters of the race. An aristocracy of talent developed, creating conflict among black leaders, a contingency which Du Bois had failed to anticipate.

Du Bois continued to believe in his main thesis, but he saw a need for a different emphasis. Du Bois (1968a) suggested that the members of the Talented Tenth had lost their focus and had become completely co-opted by white leadership, thus derailing the cultural possibilities for blacks.

The three major autobiographical works written by Du Bois (1940, 1968a, 1968b) describe the changes, and continuities, in his ideological positions over half a century. They were also significant contributions to the African American literary tradition. In these works, Du Bois demonstrated the continuing importance of the autobiography in the development of a distinct African American intellectual tradition in the United States.

Du Bois's life was influenced by history, and he became a part of that history. His leadership was an evolving one: from the Negro Academy to the Niagara Movement (with its philosophical debate with Washington) to the formation of the NAACP. The path of his life was defined by an effort to uplift his race through training and educating black leaders.

A lesson to be learned from W. E. B. Du Bois by black leaders, as well as leaders in other suppressed racial groups, is that unfailing persistence is required in order to overcome the habit and force of racism. His dedication to the necessity of a purposeful leadership for uplifting all races, particularly African American youths, was unfaltering throughout his life. Du Bois applied his talents toward solving the problems of Negroes, but he never compromised his aim, to uplift the race, in order to obtain short-term economic gains. He was focused and persistent in his aim to elevate black people in educational, social, political, and economic status to that of their white counterparts.

Du Bois's revolutionary leadership evolved from the Academy to the Niagara Movement and then into the NAACP. With the exception of in-house fighting and philosophical differences, the NAACP has proved to be more stable. Differences of opinion centered around a decision to expand membership to include non-blacks. Many of the Talented Tenth withdrew their membership in disagreement with the NAACP's policy to integrate the newly developed organization. Du Bois remained as one of its co-founding members and went on to establish *The Crisis*, which he used as a vehicle for protest against injustices against blacks and which quickly became a major voice for the black community. Today, the NAACP and *The Crisis* are still considered a focal point for historical leadership. They are an integral part of the legacy of fighting racism in America by using economic, social, and political strategies to improve the quality of life and the civil rights of all races, but in particular, for people of color.

Du Bois indicated in one of his many leadership messages that:

> We can only understand the present by continually referring to and studying the past; when anyone of the intricate phenomenon of our daily life puzzles us; when there arise political problems, religious problems, race

problems, we must always remember that while the solution lies in the present, their cause and their explanation lie in the past. (Du Bois, 1905, p. 104)

The following chapter will address my research questions and show evidence that Du Bois was a pioneer in transformational leadership. His life and work were intriguing, and his legacy has influenced the lives of African Americans and many others. I will use time frames and events out of chronological order as needed. The primary rationale has to do with the amount of untitled and unpublished manuscripts that I came across during my research in both Ghana, West Africa, and the University of Massachusetts Amherst, as well as other places in America. The following chapter will explicitly discuss data collected in West Africa and Amherst by specifically answering all four research questions.

> *Education is the whole system of human training within and without the school house walls, which molds and develops men.*
>
> ~ W. E. B. Du Bois

The Leadership of W. E. B. Du Bois

❋ Introduction

This book research was able to significantly trace Du Bois's historical writings: titled, unpublished and published from the University of Massachusetts's archive collections and rare replicas of Du Bois manuscripts and personal poetry in Ghana, West Africa. All data collected, in one way or another, discussed Du Bois's 1903 memorial address to the Talented Tenth (college graduates of Fisk University in Nashville, Tennessee; Wilberforce University of Ohio; and Atlanta University in Atlanta, Georgia). Du Bois's intention, in that address, was to challenge the college graduates to accept the responsibility of leadership and service.

Along with original manuscripts, letters, and other documents available at the University of Massachusetts, which gave insight into Du Bois's life, were a display of family portraits, artifacts that Du Bois had collected throughout his travels, as well as gifts given to him by foreign diplomats from China, Germany, and Africa. Other heirlooms that helped shed light on life in the Du Bois home (granted to the University by the Du Bois family and by his editor and friend Herbert Aptheker) were games, a shaving razor, sewing box, marriage licenses (his parents' and his own), birth certificates, his desk, ink pens, and books. This collection pointed to the early intellectual development of Du Bois's literary skills in Great Barrington, Massachusetts, where he graduated from high school in 1884.

Equally illuminating, was data collected at both the University of Massachusetts's Special Collections department in Amherst, Massachusetts and in the W. E. B. Du Bois Memorial Centre for Pan-African Culture in Ghana. The search was to find historical evidence in support of my thesis that Du Bois's idea was a pioneering conception of transformational leadership. I saw much of Du Bois's educational regalia (doctoral robes, hoods, hats, and many scholarly awards bestowed upon him from various places). Copies of framed degrees and certificates hung on the walls throughout the center. Among the most notable on-going efforts were a clearinghouse for the study of Pan-Africanism and a library for youths.

In Amherst, Massachusetts, and in Ghana, I discovered evidence of the historical factors that influenced the development of the Talented Tenth. Documents retrieved from the University of Massachusetts substantiated both Du Bois's membership in the American Negro Academy (ANA) and his strong relationship with Alexander

Crummell. Alexander Crummell, founder of the ANA, was instrumental in planting the seeds for Du Bois's later development of the Talented Tenth. This group, the Talented Tenth, overlapped with black intellectuals who were also members of the American Negro Academy.

The content of Du Bois's papers documents virtually every stage of his long career and reveals his involvement in many areas of the late 19th and early 20th century social reform movements. The earliest document in the collection was a letter to his grandmother in 1877, when Du Bois was just nine years old. Among the latest, was a draft of a letter written not long before his death, in August 1963, appealing to African American leaders to continue the struggle for human rights.

This chapter will first, discuss the historical factors that led to Du Bois's development of the Talented Tenth, and second, discuss the ethical and moral implications of the Talented Tenth. Ethical and moral values will be discussed to explain the values that helped shape Du Bois's leadership ideas and his ongoing effort to fight for racial, social, and economic justice.

This chapter will also address, under question three, the relevancy of Du Bois's ideas in solving current problems facing the African American community today. Finally, it will suggest the claim that the Talented Tenth is an integrationist theory. I will examine these claims by investigating the framework of his work, his life, and his efforts to advocate for unity of the races, and his quest for democratic inclusion.

❋ Questions

1. *What historical factors led to and influenced Du Bois's development of the Talented Tenth strategy, and what ethical and moral values are implicit within?*

Early in life, Du Bois concluded that his personal destiny was inextricably tied to the liberation and struggles of his people (African Americans) and, later, to oppressed people everywhere. Du Bois saw himself as an intellectual and activist working for the world's dispossessed and for progressive social movements in all nations. Throughout his life, Du Bois recognized the black liberation struggle as a driving wedge in all movements. Ultimately, Du Bois's life and writings illuminated the political, social, and economic development of a nation far beyond his era (Lewis, 1993, 2000).

During his high school graduation, Du Bois gave an impressive speech about Wendell Phillips, an abolitionist he admired, who died in 1884. Du Bois's presentation attracted admiration and applause from the audience of mostly parents (Agbeyebiawo,

1998). From this moment forward, he lived a very purposeful, intentional life.

Du Bois strived for the best education (Aptheker, 1985, p. 18). As a young man in his twenties, he realized the need for trained leadership to help stop the incessant acts of lynching and segregation against blacks, which he deemed not only unethical but inhuman (Hughes, 1962). When Du Bois was pleading for the development of his Talented Tenth, he envisioned college-trained graduates leading by example in order to inspire the black masses to strive for a level of equality in every aspect of private and community life (Moon, 1968, p. 56).

The Negro Academy, Du Bois's mentored relationship with Alexander Crummell, and his membership among the black intelligentsia are some of the historical factors that led to Du Bois's development of the Talented Tenth. More specifically though, Francis Broderick (1959), a Du Bois scholar, indicated that the kernel of Du Bois's idea originated while studying at the University of Berlin in Germany when he was preparing himself for his Ph.D. (which he later earned from Harvard University).

The values of honesty, truth, and justice were implicit in the idea of the Talented Tenth. Du Bois conceptualized both the past and the present largely in terms of moral dramas where conflicts of good and evil, race (literally black and white), and freedom and oppression were developed with villains and heroes. All writing was socially purposeful for him. Moreover, the story was always the same. Disciplines, genres, and methods, though important, were subordinate to the moral vision. Du Bois's moral claims were often in conflict with the context; but more importantly, they underlay the essential moral drama that shaped his texts and his ideas (Byerman, 1994). The combined beliefs of moral and economic freedom made democracy a powerful force. The idea that moral strength increases in alliances with self-interest continues here as in Du Bois's earlier works. The Talented Tenth's interests work for the good of all because they embody higher ethical and moral values (Byerman, 1994).

Du Bois's leadership ideas went beyond the color line as he strove for equality in the American social order. The publication of *The Souls of Black Folk* in 1903 and the formation of the Niagara Movement in 1905 made Du Bois the major rival to Booker T. Washington and his promotion of limiting education for black men to industrial training. This disagreement in vision prompted an ongoing historical debate between Washington and Du Bois. The publication of his book and the formation of the Niagara Movement, though, elevated Du Bois's leadership status. Later in 1909, Du Bois participated in founding the NAACP and established and edited *The Crisis* magazine, a monthly publication that gave a political and cultural voice to black Americans.

In *Dusk of Dawn* (1968b), Du Bois warned that ethical and intellectual catastrophe was in store for the United States, unless it dealt with its race problems honestly. Du Bois's early dealings with racism were dominated by a moralistic approach, which caused him to view racial prejudice as a moral deficit. According to Marable (1986), Du Bois minimized economic factors and emphasized a moral appeal for the eradication of racism. Marable (1984) also noted that Du Bois's emphasis on moral and ethical factors influenced both the academic setting and the American historiography of his time. *The Philadelphia Negro* (Du Bois, 1899) and *Darkwater* (Du Bois, 1920), both argued that blacks needed political power in order to protect their economic earnings and their right to work. The imperatives of economic independence had to be articulated within political rights. Du Bois believed that the ideals of physical freedom, political power, the training of minds, and the training of hands would be true and effective—if they could be welded into one. Du Bois's concern for excellence did not stem merely from the elitist status of the Talented Tenth but from his political sense of morality based on truth and honesty. Because the lives of so many human beings were at stake in politics, this realm could not afford to be handled carelessly (Arendt, 1958).

The advocacy of racial and social equality never implied the sacrifice of quality and excellence in government. The fundamental position of Du Bois was that education is not a matter of philanthropy, but a citizen's right. It is not a privilege based on income, but a duty of every government toward its citizens. Du Bois's critique of the ethics of education was stated as such:

> Education is not and should not be a private philanthropy: it is a public service and whenever it becomes a mere gift of the rich it is in danger. Probably the greatest threat to American education today is the fact that its great and justly celebrated private institutions are supported mainly by their graduates: Harvard, Yale, Columbia, Princeton together with smaller institutions like Amherst and Williams are increasingly looked upon as belonging to a certain class in American society: the class of the rich, well-to-do employers, whose interests are more or less openly opposed to those of the laboring million. (Du Bois, 1903c, p. 142)

On the other hand, Du Bois admitted that public or state-controlled education is not always a factor in freedom, social justice, and democratic inclusion.

Emphasis must be placed here on Du Bois's radicalism, socialism, and his high sense of pluralism, the tremendous role of his ethical vision which can be characterized more precisely as universal humanism. Du Bois's ethical vision and his sense of humility very likely came in part from his great familiarity with the Bible, which is illustrated in frequent similarities between passages or sections of his writings and Biblical books. For Du Bois, socialism was a humanist enterprise which consisted of the ideals of equality, justice, and the common good.

2. *What light does the Talented Tenth shed on the issue of how transformational leaders are created?*

Du Bois's (1903b) "Talented Tenth" theory throws a spotlight on the development of transformational leadership. Transformational leaders are created through life experience, training, and intellectual stimulation, according to Du Bois's model. In the Talented Tenth address, he talked about the importance of college training for leaders. However, he sought to use education to make the relations of men the object of their leadership. "Intelligence, broad sympathy, knowledge of the world...this is the curriculum of higher education which must underlie true life. On this foundation, [Du Bois's Talented Tenth leaders would] build breadwinning skill of hand and quickness of brain" (p. 842).

Du Bois continues, "If this be true, three tasks lay before me: first, to show from the past that the Talented Tenth as they have risen among American Negroes have been worthy of leadership; secondly, to show these men may be educated and developed; and thirdly, to show their relation to the Negro Problem" (Du Bois, 1903b, p. 842). Though Du Bois's ideas, and the manner in which they developed, were antecedent to Burns's theory of Transformational Leadership, there are similarities in Burns that reflect Du Bois's proposal of intellectual training and development to produce transforming leaders.

Burns (1978) described the intellectual leader as a devotee of ideas, knowledge, and values. A leader is a person concerned critically with values, purposes, and ends that transcend immediate needs. By Burns's definition, a leader is a person who deals analytically with ideas. He indicated that intellectual leadership is transforming (p. 142). Both Burns's and Du Bois's ideas are similarly engaging; but stated in different ways. Burns said that intellectual leaders and leadership cannot stand outside of society because they are in response to the needs of society. He named conflict as the catalyst that converts these generalized needs into specific intellectual leadership.

Du Bois (1903b) saw leaders created through emphasis on education and training, whose objectives would be service, dedication and racial uplift for the masses—to help bring about social change, freedom, and justice in America for African Americans.

Burns and Du Bois were both Harvard graduates. However, they were worlds apart in their individual, personal experiences. Burns was a political scientist who chronicled leadership styles and the lives of mostly presidents and allied leadership. Du Bois, a social and political scientist, historian, and civil rights activist, chronicled daily events of racism, inequality, poverty, and problems affecting the African American community.

While reading Burns (1978), the echo of Du Bois's life was always present. Much of what Burns talks about, so accurately describes Du Bois's existence and the model of his leadership—without ever recognizing Du Bois as a transformational leader.

Burns talks about how leaders are formed by individual, personal experience. He says, "Leadership in the shaping of private and public opinion, leadership of reform and revolutionary movements— that is, transformational leadership—seems to take on significant and collective proportions historically, but at the time and point of action leadership is intensely individual and personal" (Burns, 1978, p. 33).

Du Bois's life was dedicated to the personal battle of his own education and the use of it—he was among the best educated in America, yet his opportunities for employment were constrained by his race. Du Bois responded to this by extending his personal battle to a collective battle for the entire race. Although he did not explicitly write about the mutuality of the relationship between the Talented Tenth and the masses, he implied it through the notion of racial uplift. He saw that raising the race was necessary for the mutual benefit of all classes of black people. He became a transformational leader, and sought to train others to be leaders, with the, primarily successful, struggles of his own life as the model. Du Bois lived what Burns refers to as "conflict and consciousness" (Burns, 1978, p. 36).

Burns (1978) stated that human needs serve as a motivation by which the foundation of moral values are built. For Du Bois and black people in the United States, the driving human need was to be treated as equal. Burns felt that transformational leadership establishes the standard of morality. Du Bois lived his whole life trying to elevate America to a standard of morality in race relations.

Burns (1978) also noted that this concept of "power" in leadership is essentially a system of logical causation when there is a mutually beneficial relation between the power holder and the recipient. When the leader bases decisions and courses of action upon moral convictions, he or she is demonstrating or exercising true power. The leader must then be visionary and have a purpose in order to become a moral agent. Burns (1978) viewed transformational leaders as intellectuals, guided by ethical principles of justice and truth for human and individual rights.

Du Bois's leadership was guided by the force of his principles and his moral convictions in regard to human and civil rights, and racial, political, social, and economic injustices. Du Bois's (1903b) idea of the Talented Tenth developed from the experiences of his life and from his historical participation as a black intellectual leader. His values have helped shape the thinking of society in ways that have been transforming—through his speeches, his tireless advocacy for justice and freedom, and through the influence his writings had on his contemporaries and on those who have followed.

As a moral agent whose ethical standards and expectations of leadership are implicit within the principles of the Talented Tenth, Du Bois advocated higher education, the training of leaders, and freedom and justice for all. Du Bois's leadership strongly implied ethical and moral values. He fought almost his entire life for America to implement a democratic inclusion policy for all people.

Du Bois's leadership intentions, presented throughout his writings, his professional career, and his advocacy for social change, have conceptualized leadership in such a way that suggests racial uplift and spiritual strivings as possibly prescient to Burns's (1978) idea of transformational leadership.

Du Bois's thinking is considered, by past and contemporary scholars, to have remained consistent throughout his career. He remained focused on the ideals of higher education in America (Meier, 1966). In his attempt to establish a system for creating leaders, Du Bois advocated and pled for higher education of the Negro (Du Bois, 1903b). His progressive thoughts on the need for higher education among

African Americans were reflected in his articulation of the need for the Talented Tenth to be college educated and then to utilize their training and service to racially uplift their community. He asked, "how shall the leaders of a struggling people be trained? And the hands of a risen few be strengthened?" (Du Bois, 1903c, p. 412). He unequivocally found but one answer—the Talented Tenth (who, in our day, would be called Transformational Leaders). Du Bois asked the pertinent question, "has any nation or group risen without effective trained leadership?" (Du Bois, 1903, p. 371). He referred to education as a means to an end for political and civil rights equal to those enjoyed by white America:

> Let me illustrate my meaning partially in the matter of educating Negro youth for social power. The Negro problem, it has often been said, is largely a problem of ignorance—not simply of illiteracy, but a deeper ignorance of the world and its ways of the thought and experience of men. An ignorance of self and the possibilities of human souls. This can be gotten rid of only by training; and primarily such training must take the form of social leadership which we call education. (Du Bois, 1903c, p. 409)

Du Bois (1903c) asked, "can this training be effective without the guidance of trained intelligence and deep knowledge—without that same efficiency which has enabled modern people to grapple successfully with the problems of the submerged Tenth?" (p. 413) Du Bois clearly implied in his leadership ideas that (transformational) leaders are created through education, training, and a call to a higher (social) purpose, which is relative to Burns's (1978) notion that leaders who exhibit idealized attributes represent the highest level of transformational leadership in that their followers tend to emulate the leaders' behavior. Such leaders are authentic and have a high degree of credibility. Burns (1978) also asserted that transformational leaders are proactive in many different and unique ways.

Burns's (1978) book on transformational leadership, particularly as he discussed intellectual, transitional, moral power and transitional group leaders and "elevation," is almost synonymous to Du Bois's idea of "uplift."

The difference between Burns and Du Bois's views on leadership is primarily one of labeling. Burns coined the term "Transformational Leadership." Du Bois lived, breathed, and dedicated the entirety of his life to the same concept—not yet named in his time.

3. *How valid are Du Bois's ideas for solving current problems facing the African American community, and how valid is the claim that the Talented Tenth is an integrationist theory?*

Du Bois was a towering black scholar of the 20th century and is, posthumously, the legacy scholar of the 21st century. Long after his death in August 1963, Du Bois's work continues to influence and interest contemporary scholars. Henry Louis Gates, Jr. and Cornel West whose recent works, *The Future of the Race* (1996) and *The African American Century* (2000), and David Levering Lewis (1996, 2000) in his biographies, continue to write extensively on the life and work of W. E. B. Du Bois and the Talented Tenth.

Du Bois's writings synthesized scholarship and protest politics. Moreover, a deeper reading of Du Bois and his leadership, leads to the realization that Kwame Nkrumah and many other contemporary African leaders, Pan-African theorists, black nationalists, and civil rights activists, including Martin Luther King, Jr., Malcolm X, Thurgood Marshall, Paul Robeson, Richard Wright, James Baldwin, Langston Hughes, George Padmore, Frantz Fanon, Angela Davis, and others have been students of his writings and have followed the way paved by him, both on a theoretical level and in terms of political protest.

The depth of Du Bois's ideas on solving the "Negro problem" and how to uplift the community through the Talented Tenth have a great deal of appeal because they were formulated due to the plight of black people. Du Bois's leadership was concerned with the problems of injustice, poverty, lack of education, resources, freedom, and the need for democratic inclusion.

We can see that the Talented Tenth was an integrationist theory when examining Du Bois's notion from the vantage point of democracy. His central thoughts concerning leadership, his political affiliations, and his political actions all affirm his belief in an open, participatory democracy. Drake (1985) referred to Du Bois as a radical democrat and humanist who fundamentally believed in the basic sameness of all peoples, given certain variables. Du Bois considered himself to be working on behalf of the whole human race (p. 40). Aptheker (1971) defended the same thesis. Lester's (1971) book *The Seventh Son: the Thoughts and Writings of W. E. B. Du Bois,* characterized Du Bois as a visionary whose tremendous influence among his people was due to the fact that he was well ahead of his time. This was illustrated in his scholarship and in his civil rights activism.

The NAACP was founded in 1909 as an interracial civil rights group. Du Bois and most of the members of the exclusively Negro Niagara Movement joined others to form the first nationwide association to mount a sustained attack against the resurgent tide of racism *(The Crisis,* 1968; Gates & West, 1996; Moon, 1972; West, 1993). Du Bois had been one of the most articulate and militant leaders against the evils of segregation. In brilliant articles and searing editorials, he consistently attacked Jim Crow. Meanwhile, segregation had spread from its Dixie base and was invading, at an alarming pace, the north and west despite Du Bois's furious attacks, and the NAACP's legal efforts, intended to level the entrenched racial barriers. This is undeniable support for the notion of the Talented Tenth as an integrationist theory.

Twenty years later, on May 17, 1954, the United States Supreme Court handed down the historic decision of Brown vs. the Board of Education, which ended the constitutional sanction of segregation and sounded the death knell of the entire structure of Jim Crow. This historic event was led by one of the most notable and brightest lawyers of our times, Thurgood Marshall. It signified another victory for the NAACP. At about the same time, Du Bois, and his assembled team, completed and submitted a petition to the United Nations entitled *An Appeal to the World: A Statement on the Denial of Human Rights to Minorities in the Case of Citizens of Negro Descent in the United States of America and an Appeal to the United Nations for Redress* (Aptheker, 1985; Du Bois, 1960, 1968a, 1975).

Gates and West (Gates & West, 1996, 2000; West, 1982) raised the question of whether African Americans today have the necessary intellectual skills and existing resources available to them that will allow their leaders to confront the indescribable agony and anguish likely to be unleashed in the 21st century. Gates and West (1996) also noted that the notion of the Talented Tenth was derived from Du Bois's notion of shaping and molding the values of the masses through the managing of educational and political bureaucracies such as schools and political parties.

The question is how can black culture be preserved, and by whom? Not simply for the sake of social movements in America but for a greater world of human culture and inclusion (Gates & West, 1996, p. 166). Gates and West (1996) suggested that the remnants of Du Bois's Talented Tenth (educated middle class black people) must accept, without compromise, their historical responsibility. According to Lewis (2000), Du Bois's words were like marching orders, ingrained into the civil rights movement through the NAACP's monthly expressions in *The Crisis* in which readers received monthly installments of Du Bois's moral values. These values were reflected in Martin Luther King, Jr.'s credo that "none of us is free until each of us is free" (Gates & West, 1996, p. 22).

Indeed, today black intellectuals are as far removed from being in crisis as they have ever been. However, we must acknowledge the triumphant ascension of such intellectuals as Henry Louis Gates, Jr., David Levering Lewis, Cornel West, Manning Marable, Vivian Henderson, Stuart Gilvan, Dave Guen, Wilson Jeremiah Moses, and George Streator. Those mentioned are currently ensconced at various universities and campus communities—focused on other scholarly work and carrying out Du Bois's ideals.

One hundred years after Du Bois wrote of the Talented Tenth, we still live in an age in which political discussion about the conditions of black Americans frequently devolves into coded language about welfare dependency, crime, drug abuse, and teenage pregnancy. In this world of discourse, Richard Herrnstein and Charles Murray wrote *The Bell Curve* (1994), a scientifically bankrupt but best-selling, influential proclamation that most blacks, and poor whites for that matter, would never possess the intelligence or "genetic stuff" to become civil (Holloway, 2002). It is clear that the core concept of racial inferiority continues to shape and distort the evaluation of blacks and black intellectual works to this day (Quarles, 1996; Drake, 1967). The material quality of life for most black Americans has improved dramatically since Crummell and Du Bois's day. While not ignoring the fact that many African Americans have experienced net losses since the legal advances of the 1960s, black artistic and intellectual work is highly valued in certain areas. Intellectuals represent one of the most privileged populations in black America.

Gates and West consider themselves heirs to the Talented Tenth and therefore obliged to model a new platform reflecting Du Bois's leadership for black

America. Scholars must be guided by a vision to uplift their community, regardless of gender, race, or other descriptive attributes. This reflects the way blacks think about their own responsibility to the race. It also reflects the way white America expects blacks to think about responsibility to their race (Gates & West, 1996).

Black intellectuals have always operated in a shifting environment of crisis, whether it be the need for social uplift or the need to fight for the acknowledgement of their voices. The March on Washington in 1963, led by Dr. Martin Luther King, Jr., was an effort to inform the nation that civil rights for all people must be implemented. King's leadership was inclusive and humanistic in that he, like Du Bois, was striving for peace and brotherhood. King's movement left a historical mark on the fabric of America's history. He had become the voice of most African Americans who were victims of racism. King and his supporters were heirs to the Talented Tenth.

Much black literature declared in different eras that the "men of the race"—the Talented Tenth or the new middle class intellectuals—owe a debt of service to the black community. David Levering Lewis, professor at Rutgers University and author of two biographies on Du Bois, writes articles and anthologies, presents public lectures, and offers analytical insight that invites contemporary scholars, and others, to examine the life and work of Du Bois.

Cornel West and Henry Louis Gates, Jr. of the Harvard University Institute for African American Research have, through their writing and public speaking, gained the interest of non- African American scholars in Du Bois's propositions. Many leaders today are prompted to revisit Du Bois's leadership ideas in their attempts to resolve the persistent predicament of African Americans. Problems in African American communities exist today as they did in 1903 when Du Bois presented the findings of his first sociological research in *The Philadelphia Negro*. Du Bois's Talented Tenth are being used today to help solve problems such as unemployment, equal rights, quality education, and affordable housing in the black community. However, much work is still needed to resolve the ongoing economic, political, and social impairments in today's African American community.

Du Bois was a political pluralist who, according to Marable (1998), strongly believed in the human fellowship of diverse races and cultures as a distinct part of the Talented Tenth idea, and who realized that democratic inclusion could make this happen. He therefore conceived that democracy was incomplete. Du Bois also believed that the kinship of all human beings was not optional but a part of human nature.

Convinced that African American communities were on the verge of rapid development, Du Bois was of the opinion that one of the key problems facing

African Americans was their unfamiliarity with the ways a society organizes itself both economically and socially. Familiarity with these techniques, he said, was in effect, "social power," because not to possess them meant impotence for those who were without. Du Bois's outlook, pertaining to the qualities of an individual knowledgeable in these fields, was determined by his peculiar place in progressive thought. Du Bois (1968a), in addition to stating that African American leaders needed to be cultured gentlemen, maintained that they needed to possess positive ideals to guide them, and be familiar with "that broad knowledge of what the world knows and knew of living and loving" (Du Bois, 1903, p. 8). Only individuals meeting these criteria could be capable of leading African American communities in meeting the challenges with which Du Bois presented them—especially learning to work harder and more effectively while learning to control their emotions. Here again Du Bois's ideas for solving problems facing African American communities became more visible and clear. Du Bois challenged the Talented Tenth to rise to the occasion of leadership without being corrupted by materialism or capitalism and to preserve their racial identity in terms of its behavioral and attitudinal characteristics and traits. And he asked that they carry it into the industrial age. Leaders of this variety, Du Bois said, would bring their ideas, ideals, style, and skills to their race to shape the course of black development.

Significantly, the quality of leadership that African American communities obtain determines whether or not African Americans will accomplish their messianic purpose—giving careful attention to the education of dedicated men and women who will be unselfish and willing and able to consecrate their lives to racial progress.

Du Bois (1909, 1920) suggested that African Americans could exercise self-determination when shaping their future. Only they could choose the direction of their social, economic, and cultural development. Past experience and history made this a certainty. According to Du Bois (1931), whenever African Americans have been faced with a crisis, African American leaders capable of leading the race effectively, and dealing with the situation, appeared to take the helm. Progressive era America, in Du Bois's opinion, was just such a critical juncture in black evolution. He believed that the time had come when blacks and whites in America had to, and were going to, resolve their racial animosities.

Accordingly, African American communities required leaders who were able to guide them toward achieving racial reconciliation. Du Bois's argument required critical "social surgery in human memory" (Du Bois, 1959, p. 22). Du Bois asserted that remedies for the inequitable social arrangements would inevitably come, but he warned that the current black anger could possibly turn to rage and that a black "misguided rabble" might turn to demagogic leadership when seeking redress of their grievances. He warned that the black mass was discontented and would act soon (Du Bois, 1968a; Lester, 1971).

Concern for the economic condition of African American people, however, took precedence over the theory of racial identity in Du Bois's later writings. From the early 1930s on, Du Bois focused on the internal organization of economic life in the African American community and tried to organize "the Negro race," as he puts it, into a racial program of economic salvation along the path of peace and socialism (West, 1982, pp. 89-90). In contrast, West (1982) asserted that Du Bois presented an option, in writings and commitment, for voluntary segregation and cooperation among the black community and supported the foundation of separate institutions for blacks, such as schools and hospitals. This position, according to West (1982), was in opposition to the policy of racial integration he had advocated earlier (West, 1982).

What was the reason for Du Bois's evolution from advocacy of social and economic integration to recommending a program of a separate economy? The disastrous effects of the economic depression on African American workers and the increased racial discrimination against them in the work place (and in other areas of social life), in spite of three decades of social protest and advocacy for integration, were the major factors which determined that evolution (Bond 1980; Dennis, 1977; Gilman, 1972). In general, Du Bois supported all efforts and initiatives within the black community that could promote self-help and relative self-reliance, including the social and economic activities of black churches. Although Du Bois did not belong to a particular church denomination throughout his adult life, he never concealed his admiration for the economic power of the black church and its positive role in the advancement of black people. He paid tribute to gifted, brilliant leaders of the black church such as Richard Allen, the founder of the African Methodist Episcopal (AME) church, and Alexander Crummell whom he considered a true hero of the Negro race (Aptheker; 1985; Du Bois, 1903a; Du Bois, 1975).

The major aspect of Du Bois's appeal for racial solidarity and black self-help was his call to organize cooperative guilds and consumer societies. The idea of the Talented Tenth as a black cooperative carne up in Du Bois's agenda as early as 1903 and 1917. He utilized *The Crisis* to launch his program. Du Bois (1919) defined consumer cooperatives as "the organization of consumers into buying clubs for the object of saving the middleman profit" (p. 111). In Du Bois's writings, he discussed the need for economic improvement of the black masses and the need for a major social revolution for blacks in America. Upon this economic structure, the construction of black institutions such as the black family, church, and school were to be built.

4. *What is the significance of Du Bois's proposal of the Talented Tenth for reconceptualizing the idea of Transformational Leadership, and what can we learn from this theory?*

In the introduction to *The Autobiography of W. E. B. Du Bois: A Soliloquy on Viewing My Life from the Last Decade of Its First Century*, Du Bois affirmed his vision of himself at the age of 90 as a historical actor and a self reflective writer. He says, "This book then is the [s]oliloquy of an old man on what he dreams his life has been as he sees it slowly drifting away; and what he would like others to believe" (Du Bois, 1968a, p. 13).

Du Bois acted in numerous roles, and American society gave him a set of names which structure one's memory of him. He was a scholar, intellectual, writer, socialist, historian, and a Pan-Africanist. But his own sense of himself transcended each particular social role, and Du Bois believed that he embodied all the contradictions and paradoxes of a black man living within the African diaspora trying to regain a cultural identity.

For example, he wrote:
In the folds of this European civilization I was

born and shall die, imprisoned, conditioned, depressed, exalted and inspired. Integrally a part of it and yet much more significantly, one of its rejected parts: one who expressed in life and action and made vocal to many, a single whirlpool of social entanglement and inner psychological paradox, which seemed to me more significant for the meaning of the world today than other similar and related problems. (Du Bois, 1940, p. 3)

Du Bois's (1903) proposal of the Talented Tenth presaged Burns's (1978) idea of leadership. Through his intellectual and progressive writings and his stimulating thoughts as a visionary, new meaning had been given to leadership as we have come to know it through Burns and others. Du Bois was the first to produce an empirical study on the Negro in his sociological research *The Philadelphia Negro* (1899). In doing this study, he believed that a scientific investigation of this magnitude would provide a rational basis for social change. *The Philadelphia Negro* was also intended as a guide for the black race's social uplift. In this volume, Du Bois researched statistics that typified black life in the urban community.

Four years after writing his first sociological research, Du Bois (1903) published *The Souls of Black Folk*, where he presented a racial typology and Christian humanism. Combining both the past and the present, *The Souls of Black Folk* revealed much about

African Americans' metaphysical and sometimes anthropological state. Du Bois invoked the ambiance of black life through a collage of images, metaphors, and symbols. He later drew upon his previous work as editor and founder of *The Crisis*. From 1892 to 1963, Du Bois's leadership ideas of the Talented Tenth have influenced, expanded, and helped to shape the lives of black and white America. His work and his idea of the Talented Tenth left a legacy challenging contemporary scholars of all races to further research the truth of his ideas for racial uplift.

Du Bois's extensive scholarship has transformed leadership far beyond Burns (1978). Burns's idea is limited in its meaning and purpose and was designed to uplift mainstream society. It failed to mention or acknowledge African American leadership. What can we learn from Du Bois's leadership idea? Du Bois's idea of leadership was prophetic. It instilled pride in oneself. It was a challenge to persist and fight for what one believes is fair and just. It is a call for higher learning. Du Bois portrayed leadership as one of life's goals. The thread of Du Bois's life was linked to uplifting the masses. We can also learn that leadership is unpredictable, has many challenges, and is intended to invoke social change.

❋ *When you have mastered numbers, you will in fact no longer be reading numbers any more than you read words when reading books—you will be reading meanings.*

~ W. E. B. Du Bois

Conclusion ✻

During the progression of my historical investigation into the heart and soul of Du Bois's leadership proposal of the Talented Tenth, I came to discover that the horizon of his thoughts were much broader than I ever imagined. I immersed myself in Du Bois's writings, looking for evidence to show that he was a pioneer in the pre-conceptualization of transformational leadership. He was a pioneer in his intellectual ideas, his writings, his scholarship, and his life. He both challenged and changed the American world view in working toward resolution of the problem of racism in America. He opened the minds of African American leaders raising their consciousness to accept the responsibility of uplifting the race.

Through my examination and historical exploration, I came to realize that Du Bois's ideas are still relevant to today's leadership and that his strategy has become a legacy to the world—particularly to African American leaders and researchers. Further research is continuing among contemporary scholars who view Du Bois as a genuine thinker, whose work came to grips with the very real problems and dimensions of human existence. Du Bois's life and works were beyond his time. Many scholars have been inspired to continue the legacy of Du Bois's work. Among them are David Levering Lewis (Professor of History and the Martin Luther King, Jr. Professor at Rutgers University) who spent over 15 years examining Du Bois's life, writings, and influence; Henry Louis Gates, Jr. (Professor of History at Harvard University) who completed one of the major, historical effort of Du Bois's, the *Encyclopedia of Africana*. Others who continue working with Du Bois's ideas are: Cornel West (Professor, Historian, and Theologian at Harvard University's W. E. B. Du Bois Institute), John Bracey (Professor of History, University of Massachusetts Amherst; co-producer of "The Great Barrington" with PBS), Werner Sollors (Professor of English and Africana Studies at Harvard University). All of these scholars are striving to make Du Bois's philosophy known through their involvement with the application of his work in pursuit of the democratic ideal of social justice.

The profound impact of this extraordinary man's life became clear to me when I journeyed to Amherst, to the University of Massachusetts to study his papers in the special collection section on the 26th floor of the library, which is named in honor of W. E. B. Du Bois; when I went to Accra, Ghana and visited Du Bois's Memorial Center and examined not only his manuscripts but also the artifacts of his life; and when I went to Harlem to the Schomburg Center for Research in Black Culture. The richness of Du Bois's ideas and activities—socialism, integrationism, democratic inclusion, intellectualism, economic power, peace, justice and political rights—over the span of the late 19th century to the early- and mid-20th have definitely demonstrated several aspects of transformational leadership.

Burns stated that an intellectual is a devotee of ideas, knowledge, values, intellect and a person hovering in a particular cultural milieu or social class. By Burns's definition, this person is a theorist. One who deals with normative ideas is a moralist. A person who deals with both ideas is considered an intellectual. This notion of leadership describes Du Bois. Du Bois was a race leader, idealist, and moralist with high standards and expectations; not only for himself, but also for his followers. Du Bois's Talented Tenth were to embody a conscious purpose and respond to the needs of society, which is in keeping with Burns's transformational leadership criteria.

Intellectual leaders bring both normative and analytical ideas to bear on their environment. This is illustrated in Du Bois's classical writings, *The Souls of Black Folk* (1903), and in the Talented Tenth (1903) memorial address to the college graduates at Fisk and Wilberforce. He challenged the graduates to become leaders and to commit to uplift the spirits and minds of black people for the common good of the human race and to liberate them from the evils of the society in which they lived.

The philosophical debate and early conflict Du Bois encountered with Booker T. Washington occurred at the end of the late nineteenth century and early twentieth century. This could possibly have served as an example of the dilemma inherent in transforming leadership: how to best lead and mobilize followers for economic power and social inclusion. Washington was a short-sighted, practical leader; Du Bois was transformational.

Of all the influential eighteenth, nineteenth, and twentieth century leaders Burns mentioned to give credibility to the definition of intellectualism and intellectual leadership, he never mentioned Du Bois as one among the many heroes or ideologists. Yet Du Bois represents a prime example.

Burns (1978) mentioned African leader Kwame Nkrumah. He noted Nkrumah as being a graceful, handsome, warm, responsive voice, who viewed himself as a cross between Gandhi and Lenin in the tradition of a great thinker and politician who, like Moses, would lead his people across the Red Sea and rescue them from an imperialist massacre. Burns considered Nkrumah to be a revolutionary without a plan, a visionary, but not a builder.

Nkrumah was also a great friend of Du Bois. He was greatly influenced by Du Bois's style of transformative leadership, so much so that he invited Du Bois to come to Ghana. Du Bois did, in a self-imposed exile living out his final days in peace. He received a great deal of respect and honor from the African people, whose minds he had influenced through his leadership as an intellectual Pan-Africanist. He was invited to develop an encyclopedia of Africa, which he started, but could not finish for lack of funds. Du Bois's project was later completed by Henry Louis Gates, Jr. in the summer of 2002.

Du Bois's Talented Tenth leadership proposal supports group leadership in that its group was small and informal and their interests were clearly articulated. Du Bois's leadership model was designed for a particular group (African Americans). They were to serve and guide the 90 percent of the masses to higher levels of aspiration.

Du Bois's idea of group leadership is nonconsensual; the leader directs the followers. His definition of group and group tasks are defined by the criteria of character, education, training and unselfish commitment, which are converted to service demands. Skilled leadership moves the group to the next stage of these expectations, which in most cases is not a simple linear process. Group needs are related to resources and to the political and social climate within their own environments. However, in the case of the Talented Tenth, Du Bois was criticized for developing group leadership into a new aristocracy.

According to Burns (1978), the purpose of small groups is the achievement of these kinds of specific tasks. Group success and leader effectiveness are measured not only by the achievement of the task, but by the extent to which the task embodies group values and furthers group goals. Burns (1978) asserted that group goals may be "meaningful social participation" which are the realization of real change.

Du Bois, like others who have thought about education, concerned himself with problems relating to leadership, racism, citizenship, social conditions, economics, the balance of power, and political inclusion. But, unlike most well known educational theorists, Du Bois was a proud and sensitive black man who linked his career to blackness and to the meaning of being black in America. While he left behind no educational treatise to stand as a concise statement of his educational thought, it is possible to reconstruct his educational view from his writings, especially the "Talented Tenth" speech and those that relate to his argument with Booker T. Washington over the purpose of education.

When his educational writings and activities are examined, it becomes clear that his intellectual life was characterized by a certain ambivalence—a double consciousness. He was a vigorous black partisan and an intellectual who belonged to a thoughtful community, which transcended the confines of race. Du Bois's ambivalence resulted from his being part of the progressive intellectual current of his day and his belonging to the universe of the black American intelligentsia. It was suggested by Marable (1986) that Du Bois was mostly influenced by his environment, which was a predominantly white environment. Whether he was at Fisk, Harvard, or Berlin, the values to which he was exposed were white values. More than just his intellectual outlook was shaped by these influences. Du Bois, although black and committed to black development, chose to model his own dress and deportment after the mode which dominated the white milieu in which he had been educated. All these factors made Du Bois somewhat of an outsider in the eyes of many blacks and made him an alien in both worlds. Moreover, Du Bois was attracted by aristocracies and elites, basing his early program for black development on the education of the Talented Tenth, the black intellectual, and arguing that usually the impulse for progress within a group of people originated among its most cultivated class.

Like many progressives, Du Bois was not pleased with the influence of industrialism and the changes that it had wrought in American life. Added to Du Bois's displeasure was his dissatisfaction with American racism. While Du Bois abhorred capitalism, his critique was somewhat conservative in that it combined a desire for an uncorrupted pre-capitalistic period with an antipathy toward technology. Du Bois's ambition was to develop a program which ultimately would improve the position of blacks in the United States.

As a publicist, editor, writer, scholar, race and protest leader, Du Bois delighted in occupying center stage and commented on almost any event or discourse of interest to blacks. It was Du Bois's belief that scholarship could provide a knowledgeable basis for political and social action, which shaped many of his educational proposals. In the capacity of commentator and researcher, Du Bois made most of his comments on education and became the most prominent advocate of black higher education.

Convinced that blacks had demonstrated that they could master the same curriculum as whites, and had thus disposed of any legitimate doubts concerning their educability, he argued that justice and necessity required that blacks receive educational opportunities qualitatively equal to those available to whites. He stressed that the truth of the nation's intention toward blacks would be revealed in its educational policies toward them. He pointed out, insightfully, that questions of black humanity, economics, and politics were bound to educational practice. Throughout his career he asked blacks to accept his gospel of personal sacrifices, to cultivate their aesthetic qualities, and to improve the ambience of their society.

Education was the engine by which Du Bois was to power his political and cultural program, and higher education would ignite this engine. Du Bois specified that black colleges were to serve as active institutions. In addition to teaching, forming character, developing group consciousness, and a spirit of cooperation, they were to be the intellectual centers of the black world. They were to provide places where whites and blacks could meet in a world which otherwise kept them apart. They would be intellectual clearinghouses fostering communication among the black intelligentsia by providing havens where they might break racial barriers and move forward with the ideals of equality and justice.

A lesson to be learned from W. E. B. Du Bois by black leaders, as well as leaders in other suppressed racial groups, is that unfailing persistence is required in order to overcome the habit and force of racism. His dedication to the necessity of a purposeful leadership for uplifting all races, particularly African American youths, was unfaltering throughout his life. Du Bois applied his talents toward solving the problems of black people, but he never compromised his aim to uplift their educational, social, political, and economic status to that of their white counterparts. Du Bois (1963), in his last statement to the world said,

> One thing alone I charge you. As you live, believe in life! Always, human beings will live and progress to greater, broader, and fuller life. The only possible death is to lose belief in this truth, simply because the great end comes slowly, because time is long. (Du Bois, 1968a, p. 240)

❃ Recommendations

As a result of my historical research, I have learned that Du Bois's life work included nurturing, cultivating and developing youths for leadership and community service. Du Bois designed a visionary idea to educate and train African American youths to become socially conscious leaders, who were expected to utilize their training to uplift the impoverished and the uneducated people of the African American community. Du Bois's leadership training model was designed to train leaders to lead the masses to a level of economic self-help and liberation.

During the course of my research on the leadership ideas of Du Bois, and throughout my travels to Accra, Ghana, I observed Du Bois's Memorial Center being used as an educational foundation for youths, a place to come and learn about the leadership of W. E. B. Du Bois and the philosophy of Pan-Africanism. The example of Du Bois, and the purposeful way he lived his life, serves as a model for young people today. They will be inspired by the fact that he had to fight for his education, against a mountain of racism, and yet he used his heart, his intellect, and his leadership to get the same for black people in America.

As a result of my travels to West Africa, I founded and developed the W. E. B. Du Bois Leadership Institute for Young Scholars, targeting middle school students in grades five through seven. The program's strength incorporates academic achievement with leadership. Established in the fall of 1998, this program has served over fifty middle school youths since its inception. I have organized three educational travel experiences for the Young Scholars to visit schools in Ghana and exchange information with students of West Africa, while sharing the gifts of school supplies with students of impoverished villages. This experience alone has provided insight into other ways of living, leading and learning.

1) I recommend that universities revise their Leadership Studies curricula: first, to include the establishment of a center for the study of African American leadership. Second, to establish a program that will allow for intellectual leaders and scholars to engage in an exchange of leadership philosophies, through the sharing of a consortium of ideas and an exchange of experiences. This could be realized by inviting some of the renowned Du Bois scholars to campus. These scholars would include literati such as: Dr. John Bracey of the University of Massachusetts Amherst; Dr. Cornel West and Dr. Henry Louis Gates, Jr. from Harvard University's W. E. B. Du Bois Institute; and Dr. David Levering Lewis, the Martin Luther King, Jr. University Professor of History at Rutgers University—all of whom have written extensively on the life and works of W. E. B. Du Bois, and his

philosophy of leadership.

2) I would suggest that an inclusive revision of curricula for Leadership Studies would include establishing a five-week summer residential "Talented Tenth" program for middle school students to learn about leadership and its relationship to academic achievement. This model would be interactive with local academic and internal leadership with a required component for community service.

3) The summer program would serve as a training camp for the development of youth leadership—inspiring, enriching and encouraging academic excellence by exposing youths to campus life and the college experience. The primary focus of this type of program would include Du Bois's ideas and nurture the potential for high achievement in developing leaders. The curricula would teach problem solving and decision making strategies as training tools.

4) The effectiveness of this program in terms of growth and improvement would be evaluated after the first year of program participation and upon the return of the young people to their schools and communities. Through interviews and/or surveys of their teachers, counselors, administration,

ministers, and community leaders young scholars would be evaluated as to the level and type of leadership they have displayed in their schools and communities. The students should serve as advocates for racial and social justice and should be engaged in community service projects. The assessment aspect of the program would keep track of their progress, and data gathered would also be used to improve the program in leadership training.

5) I also recommend further study and research into the life of W. E. B. Du Bois as a model for leadership.

❋ *The worker must work for the glory of his handiwork, not simply for pay; the thinker must think for truth, not for fame.*

~ W. E. B. Du Bois

References

African encyclopedia. London: Oxford University Press, 1974.

Agbeyebiawo, D. (1998). *The life and works of W. E. B. Du Bois*. Accra, Ghana: Stephil Print Press & Co.

American Negro Academy. (1969). *Occasional papers, no. 1-22*. New York: Arno Press.

Andrews, W. L. (Ed.). (1985). *Critical essays on W. E. B. Du Bois*. Boston: G. K. Hall.

Aptheker, H. (1948). W. E. B. Du Bois: The first eighty years. *Phylon, 9*, 59-62.

Aptheker, H. (Ed.) (1951). *A documentary history of the Negro people in the United States* (Preface by W. E. B. Du Bois). New York: Citadel Press.

Aptheker, H. (1966, March). The W. E. B. Du Bois Papers. *Political Affairs, 45*, 36-45.

Aptheker, H. (1971). *Afro-American history: the modern era*. New York: Citadel Press.

Aptheker, H. (Ed.). (1973). *The correspondence of W. E. B. Du Bois, Vol. 1 Sections 1877-1934*. Amherst: University of Massachusetts Press.

Aptheker, H. (Dec. 1993). On Du Bois's move to

Africa. *Monthly Review,* 45(7), 36.

Arendt, H. (1958). *The human condition.* Chicago: University of Chicago Press, 1958.

Asante, M. K. (1988). *Afrocentricity.* Trenton, NJ: Africa World Press.

Asante, M. K. & Mattson, M. T. (1991). *The historical and cultural atlas of African Americans.* New York: Macmillan.

Bell, B. W., Grosholz, E., & Stewart, J. B. (Eds.). (1996). *WE.B. Du Bois on race and culture: Philosophy, politics, and poetics.* New York: Routledge.

Bell, D. (1992). *Faces at the bottom of the well: The permanence of racism.* New York: Basic Books.

Bennett, L., Jr. (1994, November). The NAACP's first revolt: Organization problems. *Ebony, 50,* 102-104.

Bennett, L., Jr. (1961). *Before the Mayflower: A history of Black America.* New York: Penguin Books.

Best, J. H. (Ed.) (1983). *Historical inquiry in education: A research agenda.* Washington, DC: American Educational Research Association.

Best, J. H. and Kahn, J. V. (1993). *Research in Education* (7th ed.), Boston: Allyn & Bacon.

Bond, H. M. (1925, April). Negro Leadership Since Washington. *South Atlantic Quarterly, 25,* 115-300.

Bond, J. (1980, April). Du Bois revisited. *Crisis, 8,* 145-148.

Broderick, F. L. (1959). *W. E. B. Du Bois: Negro leader in a time of crisis.* Stanford, CA: Stanford University Press.

Broderick, F. L. & Meier, A. (Eds.). (1966). *Negro protest thought in the twentieth century.* Indianapolis, IN: Bobbs-Merrill.

Brody, R. S. (1972). *W. E. B. Du Bois's Educational Ideas: a dissertation of Rutgers University.* New Brunswick, New Jersey.

Burns, J. M. (1978). *Leadership.* New York: Harper & Row.

Byerman, K. E. (1994). *Seizing the word: History, art, and self in the work of W. E. B. Du Bois.* Athens, GA: University of Georgia Press.

Childs, J. (1989). *Leadership, conflict, and cooperation in Afro-American social thought.* Philadelphia: Temple University Press.

Clifford, R. (1903, June). Cultured Negro model for race: W. E. B. Du Bois of Atlanta University: A powerful champion of colored man. *Chicago Tribune,* p. 1.

Crummell, A. (1898). *Civilization: The Primal Need of the Race* (John R. Oldfield, Ed.). Washington: The American Negro Academy.

Davis, A. (1983). *Leadership, love, and aggression.* San Diego, CA: Harcourt Brace Jovanovich.

Davis, K. E. (1982). The status of black leadership: Implications for black followers in the 1980s. *Journal of Applied Science, 19,* 309-322.

Dennis, R. M. (1977, Fall). Du Bois and the Role of the Educational Elite. *Journal of Negro Education, 46,* 388-402.

Drake, S. (1967). *Black metropolis: A study of Negro life in a northern city.* New York: Harcourt, Brace & World.

Drake, S. (1985). *Blackfolk here and there: An essay in history and anthropology.* Los Angeles: Center for Afro-American Studies, University of California.

Drinkard-Hawkshawe, D. (1977). Prelude to the Niagara movement and the NAACP. *Crisis, 84,* 53-57.

Du Bois, W. E. B. (1896). The suppression of the African slave-trade to the United States of America, 1638-1870. In N. Huggins (Ed.), *W. E. B. Du Bois: Writings [1986]* (pp. 1-356). New York: Library of America.

Du Bois, W. E. B. (1897). The Conservation of Races. *American Negro Academy Occasional Paper,* No. 2. Washington, D.C.: American Negro Academy. In Nathan Huggins (Ed.), *W. E. B. Du Bois: Writings* [1986] (pp. 815-826). New York: Library of America.

Du Bois, W. E. B. (1898a). Careers Open to College Bred Negroes In N. Huggins, (Ed.), *W. E. B. Du Bois: Writings* [1986] (pp. 827-841). New York: Library of America.

Du Bois, W. E. B. (1898b). Some efforts of American Negroes for their own social betterment: Report of an investigation under the direction of Atlanta University; together with the proceedings of the third Conference for the Study of the Negro Problems, held at Atlanta University, May 25-26, 1898. (Edited by W. E. Burghardt Du Bois.) Atlanta, GA: Atlanta University Press. [New York: Octagon Books, 1968.]

Du Bois, W. E. B. (1899). *The Philadelphia Negro: A Social Study.* Millwood, New York: Krans-Thomson, [1973].

Du Bois, W. E. B. (1901, July). The Burden of Negro Schooling. *Independent,* pp. 1667- 1668.

Du Bois, W. E. B. (1902, September). On the training of black men. *The Atlantic Monthly, 90,* 289-297.

Du Bois, W. E. B. (1903a). *The souls of Black folk.* New York: Bantam.

Du Bois, W. E. B. (1903b). The talented tenth [address delivered in 1903]. In N. Huggins (Ed.), *W. E. B. Du Bois: Writings* [1986] (pp. 842-861). New York: Library of America.

Du Bois, W. E. B. (1903c). The talented tenth. In *The Negro problem: A series of articles by representative American Negroes of to-day.* New York: J. Potts.

Du Bois, W. E. B. (1904, April). The development of a people. *International Journal of Ethics, 14,* 292-311.

Du Bois, W. E. B. (1905). Atlanta University. *In from servitude to service.* Boston: American Unitarian Association.

Du Bois, W. E. B. (1905). The beginning of slavery. *Voice of the Negro, 2,* 104-106.

Du Bois, W. E. B. (1905, October). The Negro ideals

of life. *The Christian Register*, pp. 1197-1199.

Du Bois, W. E. B. (1909). *John Brown*. Philadelphia: G. W. Jacobs.

Du Bois, W. E. B. (1911, July). Leadership. *The Crisis II*. Chicago: A.C. McClurg Co.

Du Bois, W. E. B. (1915, May). The African roots of war. *The Atlantic Monthly*, *115*, 707-714.

Du Bois, W. E. B. (1918, February). Negro education. *The Crisis*, *15*, 173-178.

Du Bois, W. E. B. (1920). *Darkwater: Voices from within the veil*. New York: Harcourt, Brace and Jovanovich.

Du Bois, W. E. B. (1920, February). On being black. *The New Republic*, *19*, 338-341.

Du Bois, W. E. B. (1922, September). Americanization. *The Crisis*, *22*, 154.

Du Bois, W. E. B. (1924). Dilemma of the Negro. *American Mercury*, *1*, 180.

Du Bois, W. E. B. (1924). *The gift of black folk: The Negroes in the making of America*. New York: Johnson Reprint [1968].

Du Bois, W. E. B. (1931, January). Education and work. *Howard University Bulletin*, *9*. Washington, DC: Howard University.

Du Bois, W. E. B. (1931, November). Moorfield Story. *The Crisis*, *38*, 392-393.

Du Bois issues call for new organization. (1934,

March 3). *Norfolk Journal and Guide.*

Du Bois, W. E. B. (1939). *Black folk, then and now: An essay in the history and sociology of the Negro race.* New York: H. Holt.

Du Bois, W. E. B. (1940). Dusk of Dawn. In N. Huggins (Ed.), *W. E. B. Du Bois: Writings* [1986] (pp. 549-802). New York: Library of America.

Du Bois, W. E. B. (1944). My evolving program. In R. Logan, (Ed.). *What the Negro wants.* Chapel Hill, NC: University of North Carolina Press.

Du Bois, W. E. B. (1968a). *The autobiography of W. E. B. Du Bois: A soliloquy on viewing my life from the last decade of its first century.* (Herbert Aptheker, Ed.). New York: International Publishers.

Du Bois, W. E. B. (1968b). *Dusk of dawn: An essay toward an autobiography of a race concept.* 1940. New York: Schocken Books.

Du Bois, W. E. B. (1969). *The conservation of races.* New York: Arno Press.

Du Bois, W. E. B. (1975). *Black folk, then and now.* (Revised edition). Millwood, NY: Kraus-Thomson.

Du Bois, W. E. B. (1985). *Against racism: Unpublished essays, papers, addresses, 1887-*1961 (Herbert Aptheker, Ed.). Amherst: University of Massachusetts Press.

Du Bois, W. E. B. (1989). *On being Black: An in-group analysis: Being essays in honor of W. E. B. Du Bois* (D. Pilgrim, Ed.). Bristol, IN: Wyndham Hall Press.

Ellison, R. (1995). *Invisible man.* New York: Random House. (Original work published 1947).

Ferris, W. H. (1913). *The African abroad: Or, his evolution in western civilization, tracing his development under Caucasian milieu.* New York: Johnson Reprint Corporation, [1968].

Ferris, W. H. (1920). *Alexander Crummell, an apostle of Negro culture.* Washington, DC: The Academy.

Ferris, W. H. (1971). The emerging leader—a contemporary view. In Rayford W. Logan (Ed.), *W. E. B. Du Bois, A Profile.* (pp. 86-121). New York: Hill and Wang.

Field. (1909). In the first edition of the *New York Age* (Newspaper Article).

Franklin, J. H. (1972). *From slavery to freedom: A history of Negro Americans.* New York: Alfred A. Knopf Inc.

Franklin, V. P. (1995). *Living our stories, telling our truths: Autobiography and the making of the African-American intellectual tradition.* New York: Scribner.

Frazier, E. F. (1928, April). The American Negro's new leaders. *Current History, 27,* 56-59.

Frazier, E. F. (1957). *Black bourgeoisie.* Glencoe, IL: Free Press.

Frazier, T. R., (Ed.). (1971). *Afro-American history: Primary sources.* New York: Harcourt Brace Jovanovich, Inc.

Gates, H. L., Jr. & West, C. (1996). *The future of the*

race. New York: Alfred Knopf.

Gates, H. L., Jr. & West, C. (2000). *The African-American century: How Black Americans have shaped our country.* New York: Free Press.

Gilman, S. C. (1972). The color line and humanism: An ethical study of W. E. B. Du Bois. *Journal of Human Relations, 20,* 397-415.

Green, D. S. (1977). W. E. B. Du Bois' [sic] talented tenth: A strategy for racial advancement. *Journal of Negro Education, 46,* 358-366.

Grimké, A. H. (1901). *Right on the scaffold.* Washington, DC: The Academy, 1901.

Hastie, W. H. (1934, January). Du Bois: Ex-leader of Negroes. *New Negro Opinion, 25.*

Henderson, L. (1970, Jan-Feb). W. E. B. Du Bois. *The Black Scholar, 1,* 45-57.

Henry, C. P. (Feb. 1992). Who won the great debate—Du Bois or Washington? *Crisis, 99,* 2.

Hoffman, F. L. (1896). *Race traits and tendencies of the American Negro.* New York: Macmillan.

Holloway, J. S. (2002). *Confronting the veil: Abram Harris, Jr., E. Franklin Frazier, and Ralph Bunche, 1919-1941.* Chapel Hill, NC: University of North Carolina Press.

Huggins, N. I., Kilson, M., & Fox, D. M. (Eds.). (1971). *Key issues in the Afro-American experience.* New York: Harcourt Brace Jovanovich.

Huggins, N. (1986). *Du Bois writings*. Cambridge, England: Press Syndicate of the University of Cambridge.

Hughes, Langston. (1962). *Fight for Freedom: The Story of the NAACP.* New York: W. W. Norton.

Jackson, B. P. (1997). The legacy of W. E. B. Du Bois. *Los Angeles Centennial, 62(52),* p. A-7.

James, J. (1997). *Transcending the talented tenth: Black leaders and American intellectuals.* New York: Routledge.

Kellogg, C. F. (1967). *NAACP, a history of the National Association for the Advancement of Colored People.* Baltimore: Johns Hopkins Press.

Lester, J. (Ed.). (1971). *The seventh son: The thoughts and writings of W. E. B. Du Bois.* New York: Random House.

Lewis, D. L. (1993). *W. E. B. Du Bois: Biography of a race, 1868-1919.* New York: Henry Holt.

Lewis, D. L. (Ed.). (1995). *W. E. B. Du Bois: A Reader.* New York: Henry Holt.

Lewis, D. L. (2000). *W. E. B. Du Bois: The fight for equality and the American century, 1919-1963.* New York: Henry Holt.

Locke, A. L. (Ed.). (1925). *The new Negro: An interpretation.* New York: A. and C. Boni.

Logan, R. W. (Ed.). (1944). *My evolving program in what the Negro wants.* Chapel Hill, NC: University of North Carolina Press.

Logan, R. W. (Ed.). (1971). *W. E. B. Du Bois: A profile.* New York: Hill and Wang.

Mandela, N. R. (1994). *Long Walk to Freedom.* New York: Brown and Co.

Marable, M. (1984). *Race, reform and rebellion: The second reconstruction in black America, 1945-1982.* Jackson, MS: University Press of Mississippi.

Marable, M. (1986). *W. E. B. Du Bois: Black Radical Democrat.* Boston: Twayne.

Marable, M. (1998). *Black leadership.* New York: Columbia University Press.

Meier, August. (1966). *Negro Thought In America 1880-1915.* Ann Arbor, MI: Ann Arbor Michigan Press.

Miller, K. (1897). *A review of Hoffman's race traits and tendencies of the American Negro.* Washington, DC: The Academy.

Miller, K. (1909). *Race adjustment: Essays on the Negro in America.* New York: Neale.

Moon, H. L. (1968, February). Leadership of W. E. B. Du Bois. *Crisis, 75,* 51-57.

Moon, H. L. (1972). *The emerging thoughts of W. E. B. Du Bois: Essays and editorials from The Crisis.* New York: Simon and Schuster.

Moses, W. J. (1978). *The golden age of Black nationalism, 1850-1925.* Hamden, CT: Archon Books.

Moses, W. J. (1989). *Alexander Crummell: A Study*

of Civilization and Discontent. New York: Oxford University Press.

Moses, W. J. (Ed.). (1992). *Destiny and race: Selected writings, 1840-1898.* Amherst: University of Massachusetts Press.

Moss, A. A., Jr. (Ed.). (1981) *The American Negro Academy: Voice of the talented tenth.* Baton Rouge, LA: Louisiana State University Press.

NAACP Board Minutes. (1913). *Papers of the NAACP: Board of Directors, Correspondence and Committee Materials; Series A: 1919-1939.* University Publications of America.

NAACP Legal Defense and Educational Fund. (1971). *An even chance.* New York: Harvard University Press.

Oldfield, J. R. (Ed.). (1995). *Civilization and Black progress: Selected writings of Alexander Crummell on the south.* Charlottesville: University Press of Virginia.

Paschal, A. G. (1971). *W. E. B. Du Bois: A reader.* New York: Macmillan.

Quarles, B. (1996). *The Negro in the making of America.* New York: Macmillan.

Rigsby, G. U. (1987). *Alexander Crummell: Pioneer in nineteenth-century Pan-African thought.* New York: Greenwood Press.

Robbins, R. (1996). *Sidelines activist: Charles S. Johnson and the struggle for civil rights.* Jackson, MS: University Press of Mississippi.

Rost, J. (1991). *Leadership for the twenty-first century.* New York: Praeger.

Rudwick, E. M. (1957, July). The Niagara Movement. *Journal of Negro History, 42,* 177-200.

Rudwick, E. M. (1960). *W. E. B. Du Bois: A study in minority group leadership.* Philadelphia: University of Pennsylvania Press.

Scarborough, W. (1903). *The educated Negro and his mission.* Washington, DC: The American Negro Academy.

Spencer, S. R. (1955). *Booker T. Washington and the Negro's place in American life.* Boston: Little, Brown.

Stewart, J. (1984). The legacy of W. E. B. Du Bois for contemporary Black Studies. *The Journal of Negro Education, 53,* 296-311.

This Week in Black History: February 23, 1868: Dr. W. E. B. Du Bois. (1995, February 27). *Jet, 87* (16), 19.

Wahle, K. O. (1968). Alexander Crummell: Black evangelist and pan-Negro nationalist. *Phylon: The Atlanta University review of race and culture, 29,* 388-395.

Washington, B. T. (1895). Mind and matter (address delivered before the Alabama state teachers' association, Selma, Ala., June 5, 1895). In *Afro-American encyclopaedia, or, The thoughts, doings, and sayings of the race: embracing addresses, lectures, biographical sketches, sermons, poems, names of universities, colleges, seminaries, newspapers, books, and a history of the denominations, giving the numerical strength of each: in fact, it teaches every subject of interest to the colored people, as dicussed [sic] by more than one hundred of their wisest and best men and women.* (Compiled and arranged by J. T. Haley). Nashville, TN: Haley & Florida, 1896, c1895: pp. 87-101.

Washington, B. T. (1901). *Up from slavery.* New York: Doubleday.

Washington, B. T. (1903). Industrial education for the Negro. *The Negro Problem.* New York: J. Pott & Co.

Watson, J. B. (1934, August). Du Bois and segregation. *The Crisis, 41,* 243-244.

West, C. (1982). *Prophecy deliverance: An Afro-American revolutionary Christianity.* Philadelphia: Westminster Press.

West, C. (1993). *Race matters.* Boston: Beacon.

Wilentz, S. (1994, April). Heart and souls: The strange education of W. E. B. Du Bois. *The New Republic, 210*(8) 14-41.

Woodard, F. (1976). *W. E. B. Du Bois: The native impulse: Notes toward an ideological biography, 1868-1897.* Dissertation, University of Iowa.

Appendix A

A Chronology and Life of W. E. B. Du Bois

From W. E. B. Du Bois, *The Autobiography of W. E. B. Du Bois: A Soliloquy on Viewing My Life from the Last Decade of its First Century*. New York, NY: International Publishers Co. Inc., 1968, pp. 396-408.

    Calendar arrangement necessarily omits whole areas of Dr. Du Bois's public life. Thus, he performed economic and sociological studies for the U. S. Census Bureau and the U. S. Department of Agriculture; he wrote weekly columns for many years in various newspapers including the *Chicago Defender*, the *Pittsburgh Courier*, the *New York Amsterdam News* and the *San Francisco Chronicle*. Dr. Du Bois delivered thousands of lectures in colleges, churches, halls, and schools in every state of the United States and in many countries of the world as Great Britain, France, China, Japan, Cuba, Haiti, Hungary, the Soviet Union, Czechoslovakia, etc. He wrote poetry that is in many anthologies; his dramatic pageants were performed before thousands in New York, Philadelphia, Washington, and Los Angeles. He helped inspire hundreds of novelists, poets, playwrights, sculptors, musicians and scientists not only by his work and example, but by direct assistance. And always he was a fighter and organizer against racism, colonialism, imperialism, illiteracy, poverty, and war. One of his earliest significant essays written while an undergraduate at Fisk in 1887 was entitled "An Open Letter to the Southern People," and was an appeal for civilized conduct and an attack upon Jim Crow; among his last acts was to inspire a protest march upon the U. S. Embassy in Accra, in August, 1963 (the month of his death), in solidarity with the historic "March for Jobs and Freedom" to Washington that month.

Du Bois's honors were many: Fellow and Life Member, American Association for the Advancement of Science; Member, National Institute of Arts and Letters; Knight Commander of African Redemption; International Peace Prize; Lenin Peace Prize; and Honorary Degrees from: Fisk University, Howard University, Atlanta University, Wilberforce University, Morgan State College, University of Berlin, and Charles University (Prague).

Timeline

1868:   February 23: Birth at Great Barrington, Massachusetts.

1883-1885:   Western Massachusetts correspondent for *New York Age, New York Globe* and *Freeman;* and Great Barrington Correspondent for *Springheld Republican.*

1884:   Graduates from high school in Great Barrington; valedictorian, speaker, subject: "Wendell Phillips."

1885-1888:   Attends Fisk University, Nashville, Tenn., receiving B.A. in 1888; teaches in country schools during summers.

1887-1888:   Chief editor of the *Fisk Herald.*

1888:   Enters Harvard as a junior.

1890:   Graduates, B. A., *cum laude* in a Harvard class of 300, is one of six commencement speakers, subject: "Jefferson Davis: Representative of Civilization" attracts national attention.

1892:   Awarded, after considerable effort, a Slater Fund Fellowship for Graduate Study abroad.

1892-1894:	Graduate student, mostly history and economics, at University of Berlin; also considerable travel in Europe.
1894-1896:	Professor of Greek and Latin, Wilberforce University, Ohio.
1896-1897:	Assistant Instructor in Sociology, University of Pennsylvania.
1897-1910:	Professor of Economics and History, Atlanta University.
1897-1911:	Organizer of the annual Atlanta University Studies of the Negro Problem; editor of their Annual Publications.
1900:	Secretary, First Pan-African Conference in England.
1905-1909:	Founder and General Secretary of the Niagara Movement.
1906:	Founder and editor of *The Moon*, published in Tennessee.
1907-1910:	Chief founder and editor of *The Horizon*, published in Washington, D.C.
1909:	Among original founders and incorporators of the National Association for the Advancement of Colored People (NAACP).

1910-1934: Director of Publicity and Research, Member, Board of Directors, NAACP.

1911: Participates in first Universal Races Congress in England.

1912: Supports Woodrow Wilson in Presidential campaign; helps organize first significant Negro break from the Republican party; resigns from the Socialist Party.

1913: Joins Editorial Board of *The New Review,* a radical, socialist-oriented magazine published in New York City.

1917-1918: Supports U. S. entry into World War; fights maltreatment of Negro troops; leads in efforts to enroll Negro officers; leads massive Silent Protest Parade (1917) down Fifth Avenue, New York City against lynchings and Jim Crow.

1919: Investigates, for NAACP, racist treatment of Negro troops in Europe; exposure creates international sensation. Chief organizer of Modern Pan-African Movement, with first conference held in Paris.

1920:	Leader in exposing U. S. role in Haiti.
1920-1921:	Founder and editor of *The Brownies' Book*, a magazine for children.
1921:	Second Pan-African Congress, London, Brussels and Paris.
1923:	Spingarn Medalist; Special Minister Plenipotentiary and Envoy Extraordinary representing the United States at the inauguration of the President of Liberia; Third Pan-African Congress in London, Paris, and Lisbon.
1926:	First and extensive visit to the Soviet Union.
1927:	Leader in so-called "Negro Renaissance" Movement; founds Negro Theatre in Harlem called the "Krigwa Players"; Fourth Pan-African Congress in New York.
1933:	Leading force in undertaking to produce an *Encyclopedia of the Negro*.
1934:	Resigns from *The Crisis* and Board of NAACP.
1934-1944:	Chairman, Department of Sociology, Atlanta University.
1936:	Trip around the world.

1940:   Founder and editor (to 1944) of *Phylon* magazine, Atlanta.

1943:   Organizer, First Conference of Negro Land-Grant colleges.

1944:   Returns to NAACP as Director of Special Research; holds this position to 1948.

1945:   With Walter White, accredited from the NAACP as Consultant to Founding Convention of the United Nations; seeks firm anti-colonial commitment on part of the United States; presides at 5th Pan-African Congress in Manchester, England.

1947:   Edits, on behalf of NAACP, and presents to the U. N., "An appeal to the World," protesting Jim Crow in the United States.

1948:   Co-Chairman, Council on African Affairs.

1949:   Helps organize Cultural and Scientific Conference for World Peace, New York City; attends Paris Peace Congress; attends Moscow Peace Conference.

1950:	Chairman, Peace Information Center; candidate in New York for U. S. Senator, Progressive Party.
1950-1951:	Indictment, trial and acquittal on charge of "unregistered foreign agent" in connection with leadership of Peace Information Center.
1958-1959:	Extensive journeys, especially to the U. S. S. R. and China.
1961:	Joins the Communist Party in the United States.
1961:	At the invitation of President Nkrumah, takes up residence in Ghana as Director of *Encylopaedia Africana* project.
1963:	Becomes a citizen of Ghana.
1963:	Dies August 27th; given a State funeral; lies buried in Accra, Ghana.

Photographs taken by this book's author at the burial place of W. E. B. Du Bois in Accra, Ghana. The inscription on the front reads: WILLIAM EDWARD B. DU BOIS 1868 - 1963. The inscription on the back reads: "W. E. B. Du Bois"…"One thing alone I charge you. As you live, believe in life. Always human beings will live and progress to greater, broader and fuller life. The only possible death is to lose belief in this truth simply because the great end comes slowly, because time is long."

I speak with no authority; no assumption of age nor rank; I hold no position. I have no wealth. One thing alone I own and that is my own soul.

— W. E. B. Du Bois

The Policy and By-laws of the Negro Academy

Du Bois's document, originally published as an undated, four page leaflet, was recently located by Dr. Adelaide Cromwell, Professor emeritus of Sociology at Boston University, among the papers of John W. Cromwell in her possession. She donated a copy to Wilson J. Moses (1989) & Alexander Crummell (1898).

The Constitution and By-Laws of The American Negro Academy were as follows:

> This Academy is an organization of authors, scholars, artists, and those distinguished in other walks of life, men of African descent, for the promotion of Letters, Sciences, and Art; for the creation, as far as possible, of a forum for intellectual taste; for the encouragement and assistance of youthful, but hesitant, scholarship, for the stimulation of inventive and artistic powers; and for the promotion of the publication of

works of merit.

Article 1 – The officers of the Academy, to be elected annually, shall be a President, four Vice Presidents, a corresponding Secretary, a Recording Secretary, a Treasurer and an Executive Committee of five persons, who shall perform the usual duties of such offices. When onerous duties are judged to demand it, the Secretaries may be salaried men.

Article 2 – The membership of the Academy shall be limited to 50 persons.

Article 3 – The conditions of membership shall be:

a) Candidates shall be men of Science, Letters and Art, or those distinguished in other walks of life.

b) Candidates must be recommended by six enrolled members, in a written application, through one of the secretaries.

c) Admission to membership shall be by ballot – by a two thirds vote of all the membership, voting in person or by proxy – due notice having been given two months before the balloting, to every member.

Article 4 – The Academy shall endeavor with care and diligence:
a) to promote the publication of scholarly works;
b) to aid youths of genius in the attainment of the higher culture, at home or abroad;
c) to gather into its archives valuable data, and the works of Negro authors;
d) to aid, by publications, the dissemination of the truth and the vindication of the Negro race from vicious assaults;
e) to publish, if possible, an "annual" designed to raise the standard of intellectual endeavor among American Negroes.

Article 5 – The Academy may invite authors and writers, members and others to submit their proposed publications to the criticism and judgment of the Academy; and if they shall receive its approval, such publications may be issued under the recommendations of the Academy.

Article 6 – The annual meetings of the Academy shall take place in the city of Washington, which shall be its seat, in the month of December, when papers shall be read, and such other exercises be held as the

Academy, from year to year, may order.

Article 7 – The admission fee to the Academy shall be $5.00 (including the first annual fee), and members shall be assessed annually $2.00. Failure in payment of which for two years shall cause membership to cease. Special assessments may be made for publications.

Article 8 – In the publications of the Academy no titles of degrees shall be joined to the names of the members.

By-Laws

1) Special meetings of the Academy may be held at the call of the Executive Committee, when and where they may decide.
2) All meetings of the Academy shall be opened with prayer.
3) Abstracts of all papers to be read before the Academy must be submitted to the executive committee before reading, and their decision regarding such papers will be final.
4) Papers and other literary productions brought before the Academy shall be limited to thirty minutes, except in cases

of the annual address by the President, to which this By-Law shall not apply.

5) Publications of the Academy of whatever kind shall be made only under authorization of the Executive Committee.

6) Foreigners of great distinction may be elected corresponding members of the Academy by a two-thirds vote of the members in attendance upon regular meeting of the Academy, on condition that such persons have been recommended by the Executive Committee.

7) Amendments to the Constitution and By-Laws may be made by a two-thirds vote of the members at any regular meeting subsequent to that in which they have been proposed.

> ❋ *Beyond the veil lies an undiscovered country, a land of new things, of change, of experiment, of wild hope and somber realization, of superlatives and italics of wondrously blended poetry and prose.*
>
> *– W. E. B. Du Bois*

Index

A

Abbott, Robert 49
abolition of all caste distinctions based simply on race and color 70
academic education 3
accommodationist 12, 46
accommodation to the status quo 60
Accra, Ghana xv, 6, 126, 134, 139, 160, 161
advocate of black higher education 132
advocates for racial and social justice 137
Africa 7, 95
African 129
African American Century, The 110
African American leadership 2, 3, 123, 135
African Communism 77
African diaspora 12
African Free School 29
African Methodist Episcopal (AME) church 120
African nationalism 7
Agbeyebiawo, D. 98

"Alexander Crummell, an Apostle of Negro Culture" 60
Allen, Richard 120
Amenia Conference 82
American Negro Academy (ANA) 46, 55, 57, 96, 97
American Negroes 4, 26, 54, 86, 103, 142, 143, 165
Amherst i, iv, xiv, 14, 15, 93, 96, 102, 126, 135, 139, 145, 150
An Appeal to the World: A Statement on the Denial of Human Rights to Minorities in the Case of Citizens of Negro Descent in the United States of America and an Appeal to the United Nations for Redress 112
Andrews, W. L. 53, 67
anti-lynching campaign 74
Anti-Slavery and Aborigines Protection Society 79
anti-Tuskegee 66

An unfettered and unsubsidized press 69
Aptheker, Herbert 13, 58, 66, 67, 87, 96, 99, 111, 112, 120
Arendt, H. 101
"A Review of Hoffman's Race Traits and Tendencies of the American Negro" 60
aristocracy of talent 90
Asante, M. K. 58
A Soliloquy on Viewing My Life from the Last Decade of its First Century 74
Association of the Study of Afro-American Life and History 59
Atlanta Compromise 35, 46, 52
Atlanta Exposition 39
Atlanta University 24, 58, 78, 95

B

Baker, Ella 26
Baldwin, James 110
Balkan War 81
belief in the dignity of labor 70
Bell, B. W. 54
Bennett, L., Jr. 53, 83
Berlin 131
Best, J. H. 2
Bible 103
black American

intelligentsia 130
black churches 120
black colleges 132
black culture 113
black intellectualism 31
black intellectuals 19
black intelligentsia 26, 88, 99, 133
Black leadership 4, 149
black liberation struggle 98
black nationalism 86
black nationalism and white liberalism 87
black pioneer intellectuals 29
Black Scholars 19
black unity 63
Blascoer, Frances 71
Blockson, Charles xiv, 15
Bond, H. M. 5, 53, 54, 70
Bond, J. 87, 120
"Booker T. Washington and the Negro's Place in American Life" 45
Boston 70
Bracey, John H., Jr. xiv, 15, 126, 135
Broderick, Francis 8, 13, 15, 76, 99, 141
Brody, R. S. 26, 87
Brown vs. the Board of Education 112
Bruce, John E. 30
Buffalo, New York 64
Bunche, Ralph 65
burial place of W. E. B. Du Bois in Accra, Ghana 161

Burns, James McGregor xi, 8, 9, 15, 16, 17, 18, 19, 104, 105, 106, 109, 122, 123, 127, 128, 130, 141
Burns's theory of Transformational Leadership 104
Byerman, K. E. 13, 58, 59, 100

C

Canal Street High School 29
capitalism 131
Careers Open to College-Bred Negroes 4
Carnegie, Andrew 53
Carnegies 41
"Cast down your bucket wherever you are," 12
Cast down your bucket where you are 37, 38
center for the study of African American leadership 135
Charles L. Blockson Afro-American Collection 14
Chicago Defender 49
Childs, J. 26
China 95
Chinese Revolution 81
Christian Pan-African concept 30
Civilization and Black Progress: Selected Writings of Alexander Crummell on the South, 1819 - 1898 32
"Civilization, The Primal Need of the Race" 56
civil rights movement 113
Clifford, R. 19, 54
color discrimination 42
Columbia University 102
communist 7, 86
community service 136, 137
conflict and consciousness 106
conflict as the catalyst 104
conflict of vision and values 50, 54
Constitutions of the South 64
controversial political agitator advocating racial equality 67
co-opted by white leadership 90
corrupted by materialism or capitalism 117
Council of African Affairs 87
crisis of black leadership 47
Crummell, Alexander 26, 28, 32, 33, 43, 46, 54, 55, 56, 57, 59, 88, 96, 97, 99, 114, 120
Crummell, Boston 29

cultural relativism in
American society 88
"cure" for color prejudice
11
current problems facing
the African American
community 2, 97,
109

D

Darkwater 82, 101
Davis, A. 5
Davis, Angela 110
Davis, K. E. 54
democratic inclusion 116,
127
Dennis, R. M. 120
Department of Special
Collections and
University Archives
i, iv, xiv
development of the
Talented Tenth 96
development of
transformational
leadership 103
Diocese of Massachusetts,
Episcopal Church
29
disenfranchisement of
black people 42
distinction between race
and culture 88
Douglass, Frederick 48
Drake, S. 111
Drinkard-Hawkshawe,
Dorothy 61, 63, 64
Du Bois Memorial Centre

for Pan-African
Culture 7
Du Bois's ethical vision
102
Du Bois's lack of training
in business
management 79
Du Bois's Memorial Center
126, 134
Du Bois to Villard
correspondence 84
Du Bois, W. E. B. i, ii, iv,
vi, vii, viii, ix, x, xi,
xiv, xv, xvi, 1, 3, 8,
10, 12, 13, 16, 21,
22, 23, 24, 31, 32,
33, 34, 39, 40, 41,
42, 43, 44, 47, 48,
49, 50, 51, 52, 53,
54, 55, 56, 57, 60,
61, 63, 64, 65, 66,
67, 68, 70, 71, 87,
90, 91, 94, 95, 96,
98, 99, 100, 101, 102,
103, 104, 106, 107,
108, 109, 110, 111,
113, 114, 115, 116,
117, 118, 119, 120,
121, 122, 124, 125,
126, 128, 130, 133,
134, 135, 136, 137,
138, 139, 141, 142,
143, 145, 146, 147,
148, 149, 150, 151,
152, 153, 162, 168,
169
due process of law 73
Dusk of Dawn 101

E

economic life in the African American community 119
economic power 127
economic power of the black church 120
economic self-help and liberation 134
educated Negro leader 9
educational leadership 8
elevation 109
elitist 4, 5, 32, 101
Ellison, Ralph 61, 84
empowerment of followers 16
Encyclopedia of Africana 55, 126
England 7
Equality and education 39
equality between the sexes 12
ethical and moral implications of the Talented Tenth 97
ethical principles of justice and truth for human and individual rights 106
ethics of education 102
Eurocentric perspectives of leadership 9
exchange of leadership philosophies 135
exclusion of African Americans from the leadership curriculum 8
exploiters of the race 90

F

failure of accommodationism to produce results 50
Fallinwider, S. P. 15
Fanon, Frantz 26, 110
Federation 62, 63
Ferris, William H. 39, 42, 43, 54, 60, 65
Field 42, 49
Fifteenth Amendment 64, 73
first African American to receive a doctoral degree 10
First World War 81
Fisk University 10, 95, 127, 131
Fort Erie 64
fourteenth and fifteenth amendments 62
France 7
Franklin, J. H. 51
Franklin, V. P. 23, 30, 31, 32, 59
Frazier, E. F. 34, 39, 48, 49
Frazier, T. R. 75
Freedom of speech and criticism 69
Freedom's Journal 48

G

Gandhi 128
Garvey, Marcus 34, 51
Gates, Henry Louis, Jr. 3,

4, 13, 15, 28, 46, 48,
110, 111, 112, 113,
114, 115, 116, 126,
129, 135, 146
General Secretary of the
Niagara Movement
66
genetic stuff 114
Germany 7, 95, 99
Ghana, West Africa xv, 6, 7,
14, 93, 95, 96, 126,
128, 134, 135, 139,
160, 161
gifts of school supplies
with students of
impoverished
villages 135
Gilman, S. C. 120
Gilvan, Stuart 113
"Gospel of Work" 43
Grandfather Clauses in
Southern State
Constitutions 64, 73
Great Barrington,
Massachusetts 96
Great Debate 34
"Great Man Theory" of
leadership 8
Green, D. S. 1, 85
Grimké, Archibald H. 60
Grimké, Francis J. 56
Guen, Dave 113

H

Harlem Renaissance 59
Harpers Ferry 70
Harvard's Historical Series
11

Harvard University 3, 10,
11, 25, 41, 49, 99,
102, 104, 116, 126,
131, 135, 150, 155
Harvard University Institute
for African American
Research 116
Harvard University's W. E.
B. Du Bois Institute
126, 135
Hastie, W. H. 19
heirs to the Talented Tenth
115
Henderson, L. 5
Henderson, Vivian 113
Henry, C. P. 51, 70
Henry Street Settlement 71
Herrnstein, Richard 114
Hicks, Charity 29
higher education and
community service
88
higher education in
America 107
higher education of the
Negro 107
higher ethical and moral
values 100
highest and best human
training as a
monopoly of no
class or race 70
historical research in
education 1
Holloway, J. S. 114
Hope, John 59
Howard University 30
How shall American
Negroes be

emancipated from economic slavery? 86
Huggins, N. 54, 84
Hughes, Langston 76, 99, 110
humanitarian 12

I

idealist 127
ideological controversy between Du Bois and Booker T. Washington 11
industrial education 3, 39, 40, 50, 53, 59, 60
inner Negro cultural ideal 77
integrationism 127
integrationist viii, 3, 12, 51, 97, 109, 111, 112
integrationist theory 97, 109, 111, 112
integration of the races 9
intellectual and moral leadership 9
intellectual centers of the black world 133
intellectualism 127
intellectual leaders 18, 127
intellectual Pan-Africanist 129
Interlibrary Loan Department of the Copley Library xiv
interracial conference 71
Interstate Commerce Clause of the Constitution 64

J

Jackson, B. P. 77
Jackson, Reverend Jesse 35
James, Joy 25
Jet Magazine 77
Jim Crow 50, 111, 112
Johnson, James Weldon 59
Jones, John H. 61
Journal of Negro History 69
justice 127

K

Kahn, J. V. 2
Kellogg, C. F. 84
King, Martin Luther, Jr. 6, 110, 113, 115
Know, George L. 61

L

leader directs the followers 129
leaders are formed by individual, personal experience 105
Leadership 16
leadership and power as a source of relationship 17
leadership by a college educated elite 44
leadership of W. E. B. Du Bois 134
leadership paradigm 4
leadership strategies 5, 13
Leadership Studies 1, 2, 7, 8, 9, 13, 15, 135,

136
Leadership training 7
legacy to the world 125
Legal Defense Fund 77, 86
legal defense of Negroes and Negro rights 73
legal rights 75
Lenin 128
Lester, J. 24, 51, 68, 111, 119
Lewis, David Levering 3, 9, 13, 15, 48, 65, 80, 85, 98, 110, 113, 115, 126, 135, 148
Liberia Records of Letter 30
Liberia, West Africa 30, 59
Library of Congress iv, xiv, 14
Lincoln Institute 11
Lincoln Memorial Church 57
Locke, Alain 55, 59
Logan, R. W. 15, 50, 51, 84, 87

M

Malcolm X 110
Mandela, N. R. 24
Manhood suffrage 69
Marable, Manning 101, 113, 116, 131
March on Washington 6, 115
Marshall, Thurgood 110, 112
Meier, August 29, 107
Milholland, John 71
Miller, Kelly 45, 60, 76

modern African American protest 66
Monrovia 30
Moon, H. L. 8, 24, 51, 99, 111, 149, 156
moral drama 100
moralist 127
morality based on truth and honesty 101
moral vision 100
Morehouse College 59
Morris, E. H. 61
Moses, Wilson Jeremiah 113
Moses, W. J. 31, 32, 34, 88
Moses would lead his people across the Red Sea 128
Moss, A. A. 58, 59
Murray, Charles 114

N

NAACP's board minutes 84
Nashville, Tennessee 10
National Association for the Advancement of Colored People (NAACP) 27, 61, 70, 71, 92, 100, 111, 112, 113
National Council of Social Agencies 82
National Federation of Colored Men of the United States 61, 62
National Negro Committee 71

National Race Commission 81
Nation of Islam 51
Negro Academy 27, 31, 54, 60, 88, 91
Negro art and literature 82
Negroes 1, 2, 3, 4, 5, 9, 23, 24, 26, 39, 41, 42, 44, 48, 49, 51, 54, 69, 70, 73, 74, 80, 81, 82, 83, 86, 91, 103, 142, 143, 144, 147, 165
Negro Press 48
Negro problem 9, 26, 27, 35, 69, 72, 73, 108, 110, 143
new and great Negro ethos 87
new aristocracy 129
new leadership class 3
New York Age 49
New York Globe 10
Niagara Falls, Canada 64, 65, 89
Niagara Movement 61, 62, 63, 65, 89, 91, 92, 100, 111
Nkrumah, Kwame 6, 110, 128
nonconsensual 129
"none of us is free until each of us is free" 113
northern capitalists 39
North Star 48

O

"Of Mr. Booker T. Washington and Others" 39, 40, 52
"Of Our Spiritual Strivings" 47
Oldfield, John 32, 33
Oneida Institute 29
ongoing historical debate between Washington and Du Bois 100
Operation Push 35
Ovington, Mary White 70, 84

P

Padmore, George 110
Pan-Africanism 12, 96, 134
Pan-Africanist 7
Paschal, Andrew 15, 57
peace 127
Phillips, Wendell 98
Photographs taken by this book's author 161
pioneering conception of transformational leadership iv, xii, 96
pioneering educational and leadership efforts 10
Point Pleasant, New Jersey 31
political rights 127
Powell, Colin 35
pre-conceptualization of transformational leadership 125
preserve their racial identity

117
Princeton University 102
"principle oneness" 30
principles of human
    brotherhood 70
Prints & Photographs
    Division iv
problem of the color line
    20
problem people 47
problem solving and
    decision making
    strategies as training
    tools 136

Q

Quarles, B. 58, 114
Queens College 29
quest for democratic
    inclusion 98

R

"Race Adjustment" 45, 76
race leader 88, 127
Race Matters 46
race prejudice as a
    fundamental fact 43
Races Conference 80
"race spirit" 44
racial equality 7, 13, 23,
    67
racial inferiority 114
racial prejudice as a moral
    deficit 101
racial progress 118
racial reconciliation 118
racial uplift 104, 105, 123
racism 3, 34, 65, 88, 90,
91, 92, 101, 105, 111,
115, 125, 130, 131,
133, 134, 140, 145,
154
relationship between
    economics and
    political power 51
relevancy of Du Bois's ideas
    in solving current
    problems 97
remedies for the Jim Crow
    laws 68
Renaissance of Negro
    Literature 83
residential segregation laws
    and ordinances 73
resolving the problem of
    racial inequality 9
responsibility without
    power 16
right of Negroes to sit on
    juries 73
"Right on the Scaffold, or
    the Martyrs of 1822"
    60
Rigsby, G. U. 28, 32, 33
Robbins, R. 114
Robeson, Paul 110
Rockefeller, John D. 53
Rockefellers 41
Roosevelt, Theodore 66, 81
Rost, J. 9, 151
Rudwick, E. M. 65, 66, 67,
    69, 70, 76
Russia 7
Russworm, John 48
Rutgers University 115,
    126, 135

S

San Diego State University Special Collections & University Archives xv
Scarborough, W. 19, 33, 39
Scarborough, William S. 60
scholarship could provide a knowledgeable basis for political and social action 132
Schomburg Center for Research in Black Culture xiv, 14, 126
segregate primary elections race 73
self-help program of economic organization along racial lines 86
service was the ideal of leadership 6
sixth amendment 62
social benefit 1
social change 1, 13, 87, 104, 107, 122, 123
socialism 103, 127
social power 117
social reform movements 97
social regeneration 16
Social Sciences Department of the Library of Congress xiv
Sollors, Werner 126
Southern Cotton Exposition 35
Special Collections 96
Spencer, Samuel 45
Spingarn, Joel V. 81, 82, 85
standard of morality 106
Stewart, J. 85
Storey, Moorfield 71
Straker, David Augustus 61, 62, 63
Streator, George 113
Supreme Court 64
Sween, W. Allison 61

T

Talented Tenth iv, vii, viii, xi, xii, 1, 2, 3, 4, 5, 6, 8, 12, 14, 15, 17, 23, 24, 25, 26, 27, 28, 33, 35, 42, 51, 54, 55, 58, 59, 66, 67, 68, 69, 70, 77, 78, 89, 90, 92, 95, 96, 97, 98, 99, 100, 101, 103, 105, 106, 107, 108, 109, 110, 111, 112, 113, 114, 115, 116, 117, 120, 121, 122, 123, 125, 127, 129, 130, 131, 136
Talented Tenth as a black cooperative 120
Talented Tenth leadership proposal 129
"Talented Tenth" speech 130
Temple University xiv, 14, 15, 141
Temple University Library 14

ten percent xi, 1
The Autobiography of W. E. B. Du Bois: A Soliloquy on Viewing My Life from the Last Decade of Its First Century 68, 121
The Bell Curve 114
the black intellectual 131
the color line 85, 100
The Conference of the Negro Problem 58
"The Conservation of Races" 44, 56, 60
The Crisis 45, 72, 92, 100, 111, 113, 120, 123
"The Educated Negro and His Mission" 60
The Future of Africa 31
The Future of the Race 110
The Gift of Black Folk 82
"The Great Barrington" 126
The Greatness of Christ 31
The Guardian 49
The Horizon 45
"the most ingenious invention for human progress" 44
The Negro Academy 99
the Negro Problem 9, 104, 108, 152
The New Negro 83
The Niagara Movement 27, 64
The Philadelphia Negro 11, 57, 101, 116, 122
The Progressive party 80
The Relations and Duties of Free Colored Men in America to Africa 31
These United States 83
The Seventh Son: the Thoughts and Writings of W E. B. Du Bois 111
The Souls of Black Folk 3, 28, 40, 47, 49, 52, 100, 122, 123, 127
The Suppression of the African Slave Trade to the United States of America: 1638-1870 11
The Talented Tenth 4, 5, 15, 23, 25, 26, 100
The Task for the Future-A Program for 1919 75
third party movement 81
Thomas, Clarence 35
transformation xi
transformational leaders 106, 108
transformational leadership iv, viii, xi, xii, 1, 2, 3, 10, 14, 15, 17, 83, 93, 96, 103, 104, 105, 106, 107, 109, 121, 125, 127
transformative leadership 128
Trotter, Monroe 46, 49, 67
Tuskegee Institute 3, 11, 40, 53
"Tuskegee Machine" 12, 68
Tuskegee Normal and Industrial Institute 39

Tuskegee University 40

U

"Uncle Tom" 12
United effort to realize these ideals under wise and courageous leadership 70
United Nations 112
unity of the races 98
universal humanism 102
University of Berlin 10, 99
University of Cambridge 30
University of London 80
University of Massachusetts 95, 96
University of Massachusetts Amherst i, iv, xiv, 15, 93, 126, 135
University of Pennsylvania 57
University of San Diego xiii, xv
University of Southampton 32
uplift 109
uplifting the American Negro 3
uplifting the race 125
uplift the race 1, 91
Urban League 78
U. S. Supreme Court 73

V

Villard to Garrison correspondence 84
visionary 46
voluntary segregation and cooperation among the black community 119

W

Wahle, K. O. 29
Walling, William English 71, 74
Washington, Booker T. viii, xi, 3, 11, 26, 27, 31, 34, 35, 38, 39, 40, 41, 45, 46, 47, 48, 49, 50, 51, 52, 53, 55, 59, 60, 62, 65, 66, 79, 82, 87, 88, 90, 100, 128, 130, 151
Washington, D.C. 57
Washington's theory of Industrialism 89
Watson, J. B. 85
Watts, J. C. 35
W. E. B. Du Bois Department of Afro-American Studies xiv
W. E. B. Du Bois Leadership Institute for Young Scholars 134
W. E. B. Du Bois Library i, iv
W. E. B. Du Bois Memorial Centre for Pan-African Culture xv, 96
Wells, Ida B. 26, 84
West Africa 85, 93, 134,

A Pioneering Conception of Transformational Leadership | 181

135
West, Cornel xiv, 3, 4, 13,
  14, 15, 20, 28, 30,
  34, 46, 47, 59, 78,
  85, 93, 95, 110, 111,
  112, 113, 114, 115,
  116, 119, 126, 134,
  135, 146, 152
western acquisitive society
  78
white philanthropists 41
white power structure xi
wikimedia commons iv
Wilberforce University 11,
  95, 127
Wilentz, S. 12

Williams 102
Wilson, Woodrow 81
Woodard, F. 13
Woodson, Carter G. 55, 59
World War 82
Wright, Richard 110

X

Y

Yale University 102

Z

About the Author

Dr. Ella Sloan is a native Texan. A life long learner with multiple leadership skills and talents, Dr. Sloan believes that life experience is the best teacher. She earned her Doctorate in Educational Leadership from the University of San Diego, and both her Master's and Bachelor's degrees from San Diego State University. She has managed to blend her vocational and academic talents into an inspired and inspirational professional career. Her leadership has benefited her community, church, and especially young scholars, whose lives she has had the opportunity to influence, and whom she has watched grow into bright academicians, teachers, businessmen and businesswomen with promising careers across this country.

Dr. Sloan is a recipient of numerous leadership awards, and has served many organizations in a myriad of capacities. Such organizations as the NAACP, National Sorority of Phi Delta Kappa, Inc. (holding both regional and national offices), and AARP (being a local and state volunteer of the San Diego local chapter) are the back drop and landscape of her continued dedication to being a voice and presence in and beyond her community. As a former business owner in San Diego, California for over 18 years, she has always carried a passion and thirst for knowledge, and has vied to make that knowledge available as a catalyst for change. She believes in living life fully, and being thankful for all blessings.

Production Notes

Throughout this book, I attempt to use the term African American without hyphenation. However, where it appears as part of a direct quote, I include the hyphen in order to remain true to the original author's style and intent.

The primary font used in this book is the ITC Giovanni family. For the W. E. B. Du Bois quotations Melany Lane font was chosen to evoke a sense that Dr. Du Bois himself might have handwritten these words that still ring clear and true today.

Quotations ✻

Quotations of W. E. B. Du Bois are used for inspiration and visual emphasis throughout this book. This list provides the first line of each quotation and the page on which it is found.

Now is the accepted time	Cover
All men cannot go to college	ii
A classic is a book that doesn't have to be	iv
It is the trained, living human soul,	vi
There is in this world no such force	x
Believe in life!	xvi
Art is not simply works of art;	21
The cost of liberty is less	22
Education is the whole system of human	94
When you have mastered numbers,	124
The worker must work for the glory	138
I speak with no authority;	162
Beyond the veil lies an undiscovered country,	168

www.ingramcontent.com/pod-product-compliance
Lightning Source LLC
Chambersburg PA
CBHW050841040426
42333CB00058B/211